HOLY LOVE

Essays in Honor of Dr. M. William Ury

Foreword by Dr. John N. Oswalt
Diane N. Ury, Editor

With Thomas H. McCall, David Buschart, Roger J. Green,
Victor Hamilton, Dennis F. Kinlaw, and others

Printed in the United States of America

For information, write:
The Salvation Army
USA Southern Territory
Literary Council
1424 Northeast Expressway
Atlanta, GA 30329

ISBN: 978-0-86544-498-0

Contents

Foreword

I FIRST MET Bill Ury when he was a student at Asbury Theological Seminary, and I was a young professor. He was one of several bright, eager, and obviously committed students that I invited to join a small group that met in my seminary office once each week. Part of my reason for creating these groups was so that students who bore the mark of being used by God in coming years could know something of the inner life of a (hopefully) admired faculty person. So, the opening sessions of the group each year were devoted to the sharing of stories. Bill's story was gripping. Growing up in Taiwan, the son of a beloved father, who was often away in missionary work, and of a mother who was passionately concerned for the spiritual life of her children, Bill had clearly absorbed some of the commitment of his father and the passion of his mother. By the time I knew him, he had weathered teen-aged rebellion and was deeply engaged in becoming a man of God.

After that initial encounter, very rewarding for me, our paths diverged. When next I met Bill, we were both faculty members at Wesley Biblical Seminary in Jackson, Mississippi. Bill had completed a doctorate at Drew University and had been teaching systematic theology at Wesley for some time before I joined the faculty there. One of the first things I learned when I arrived was that Bill Ury was the favorite professor of almost all the students. The other members of the relatively small faculty were all competent and effective, but Bill was the one to whom the students gravitated. If a student was going on for further study, and I asked him or her what discipline they were going to pursue, it was invariably systematic theology. That commitment and passion that I had recognized in him as a student had come to full flower in the classroom. Along with the passion and commitment, the students loved his humor, his way of making the material relevant to life, and his genuine concern for them and their lives.

I have also had the opportunity to know Bill as a preacher. I had the privilege of being the president of a camp meeting for a decade. When I arrived in the position, I discovered that Bill had preached there in the ten-day meeting a couple of times previously and was scheduled to return in the future during my tenure. From my previous experiences with Bill, I was pleased to discover this. When his scheduled assignment arrived, I listened to him preach once each day with deepening appreciation. Bill Ury is a preacher of the Word. His sermons are solidly rooted in the Scripture and in careful and faithful interpretation of the Word. But good Bible lecturers can do that. Bill goes beyond that with clear, relevant, intellectually rich applications of the biblical truth to modern life. With all of that, he has the ability to hold the congregation's attention through the use of personal illustrations and humor. Needless to say, he has been regularly invited to return to the pulpit of that camp meeting.

Finally, I have known Bill in the context of theological discussion and debate. He and I have been part of a group of theologians and biblical scholars who are attempting to put together a collaborative systematic theology text. Each of us was assigned a topic to write upon, then our work was circulated to the rest of the team for their comments and suggestions, often resulting in a second draft that was circulated. Then once or twice a year the entire team met for a long weekend to discuss the contributions received since the previous meetings. These meetings were wonderfully stimulating and sometimes vociferous. Bill's work on Christology was a model in its thoroughness and its penetration. In the discussions, Bill was always engaged, but he was also concerned that all voices be heard and that any ruffled feelings be addressed and cared for. In that setting his essential humanity was very apparent.

In summary, Bill Ury is a capable scholar, a gifted communicator, a man with a heart for others, a passionate and committed Christian. This volume is a fitting honor to such a man.

— Dr. John N. Oswalt, *Distinguished Professor of Old Testament, Asbury Theological Seminary*

For over two decades Dr. William Ury has been a consistent proclaimer of biblical holiness to the ranks of The Salvation Army. He is steeped in the classic holiness literature of his heroes of the holiness movement; John Wesley, Samuel Logan Brengle, Catherine Booth and Dennis Kinlaw.

I first heard Bill speak at The Salvation Army's Southern Bible Conference at Lake Junaluska. The zest and passion of his teaching was the result of his dedication to the love and study of God's Word.

Bill makes Jesus Christ the center of his life's work and study. His holiness messages are powerful and convincing expositions of Holy Scripture as seen in the life of Jesus Christ for today. For God's people to understand Him requires knowing His Word and then allowing His Word to dwell in them richly. The primary thrust of Bill's ministry is to make God's living Word known to His people.

I have found Bill to be a humble servant of God. He has a winsome and wholesome sense of humor. He often will poke fun at himself. The Jesus he knows is the Christ of the wedding feast who knew how to laugh and enjoy good fellowship. His relationship with Jesus is filled with joy and laughter.

He is quite aware of the depth of his own unrighteousness and his deserving of God's wrath. And as such he revels in the unmerited grace and mercy of God.

In my opinion, he is the best teacher of biblical holiness. Every time I have heard him, his teaching has been outstanding. He has had a profound impact on the lives of so many in The Salvation Army, including myself.

Bill has been a favorite at the Southern Bible Conference. Over the past twenty-five years he has taught there several times. The delegates at the conference are a diverse group. There are senior Salvation Army officers in leadership positions, local corps officers (ministers), local lay leaders, soldiers (members), and retired officers of The Salvation Army in attendance. In addition, there is a large group of 250 plus men and women in recovery from substance abuse. To this wide spectrum of listeners, Bill is able to communicate effectively through the power of the Holy Spirit. Often there are many kneeling at the penitent form at the conclusion of his teaching. God has used him greatly. He has the gift for understanding and interpreting the Word of God unlike anyone else I know. Those who have sat under his teaching have grown in relationship with the Lord.

Second only to Jesus, Bill loves his family. He is devoted

totally to Diane and always has her best interest at heart and often speaks of her with the highest regard. Diane has consistently been supportive of Bill's ministry which often meant staying at home with the children when Bill traveled to various teaching invitations. Bill loves his children and is so proud of their accomplishments and of their love and service to the Lord. He is also a very proud grandfather.

Once when I was with Bill at an officers' councils in Florida, he shared he and Diane were going to pastor an Evangelical Methodist Church in North Carolina. I said to him I wish I had known, as I would have had a position for him in The Salvation Army.

A couple years later my wife, Barbara, met Diane at a women's conference. Barbara said to her how much we thought Bill was an undercover Salvationist and he and she would fit well in our ranks. Diane said not to give up on that thought.

A few years later I was able to offer them a position. We were happy to engage both Bill and Diane in a full-time ministry role as National Ambassadors for Holiness, a position similar to what Commissioner Samuel Logan Brengle filled a century ago. Both Diane and Bill have made The Salvation Army their church home.

The Urys have ministered together in local Salvation Army corps across America, Salvation Army officers' councils, and holiness retreats. They serve at the Brengle Holiness Institute in Chicago, and the National Seminar on Evangelism and National Seminar on Holiness. They also have taken engagements in territories outside the United States. Heaven will only know the impact Dr. William and Diane Ury have had on The Salvation Army.

— Commissioner David Jeffrey, *National Commander of The Salvation Army USA, retired*

Preface

I SUPPOSE ONE of the first inspirations for this *festschrift* for Bill Ury came immediately following church worship service one Sunday morning in Elizabeth City, NC. One of Bill's former students and a member of his discipleship group while at Wesley Biblical Seminary had surprised us by bringing his wonderful family to our church while they were passing through on vacation. They had just picked up their children from our children's ministry wing and we were hugging and greeting one another with surprised joy. Then I saw it. The youngest child in Nathan's arms still had his nursery name tag adhered to the back of his shirt. It said, "Ury." When I asked if Ury truly is their son's name, they answered only with magnificent smiles. No other explanation was offered. Or needed.

For several years I've dreamt of creating a *festschrift* in honor of Bill's ministry. After he'd been teaching at Wesley Biblical Seminary for many years, I began to make note of the number of his students, and others, who were deeply impacted by his academic influence in their lives in the range of historical and systematic theology, trinitarian, and Wesleyan Theology. But Bill's life of scholarship has been exceptional because of the way it was never separated from his commitment in his personal life to pursue living the reality of holy love. As an evangelist, pastor, and lay person in the church, he deeply valued the power of the preached Word, theologically informed pastoral ministry, and discipleship. Dozens of businessmen, as well as seminarians and scholars, have been formed spiritually by Bill's personal life. Also, his immediate family lived under not only his teaching ministry, but his faithful holy love in the home. Many of these former students and friends now serve all over the world in capacities of faithful and significant ministry, as professors, bishops, missionaries, pastoral theologians, and godly businesspeople. Much of who they are is an outflow of Bill's presence in their lives at some time.

My vision for this collection is that it will reflect this remarkable kind of scholar — a brilliant and hard-working academician, a faithful lay person and Sunday school teacher in the local church for twenty years, a holiness camp meeting preacher, a pastor of a small rural church, a friend who's a disciple maker, and a loyal nourishing husband and father. To only feature "scholars" in a book that is to honor Bill Ury is missing the mark, in my mind. When I researched the definition of *festschrift*, I found that it's a book to honor the life of a scholar, with contributions from "friends, former students, and colleagues." Within these pages you will find this variety of contribution reflecting the fullness of the kind of man they're intended to honor. I realize it might be a bit different than some *festschrifts*. But I think Bill is a bit different from the average scholar. This, I believe, will encourage seeking holy love within the hearts and minds of all who will read it.

Beyond recognizing Bill Ury's contribution to the Church, that is the point and purpose of this volume. Clearly, our world and indeed the Church itself, is in deep need of the presence of holy love pervading every part — unchanging righteousness and truth that abide within other-oriented love. Then the meaning of human existence is sourced in the wellbeing of others rather than in self. In these essays you will gain understanding of holy love through an array of topics, expressed through individuals who live in submission to holy love Himself and long to reflect His nature. My prayer is that you, dear reader, will know this for certain: you are made for this. To be a person filled with and manifesting the holy love of the triune God is the intention of the Creator for you. God intends to make this real in your daily life and ministry. You can be a person whose commitment in your personal life is to pursue living the reality of holy love. And when we do, that is what will change the world.

Introduction

THE MAIN PURPOSE of this volume is to offer exposure to ideas about the triune God's nature of holy love. What does "holy love" mean for us? One of God's most frequent commands to us is to be holy as He is, and to love as He loves. This book will integrate those commands into the thoughtful disciplines of the Church.

Bill Ury rarely, if ever, teaches or preaches a message without using the phrase, "holy love" in some context therein. For him, it is ultimate reality. Therefore, the title of this *festschrift* is *Holy Love*. I offered each contributor the prompt, "Holy Love and…" In this collection of essays we will read about holy love as it relates to particular theological, biblical, historical, pastoral, and missional realities such as: the nature of the triune God, the nature of Creation, of human nature, and the Church at present and in its history.* You will gain understanding of holy love through an array of topics, expressed through respected thinkers whose callings professionally and personally have long compelled them to seek holiness.

---

* Chapter Ten, "Holy Love and Church History: The Curious Case of Edward Irving," revises "Edward Irving on Christ's Sinful Flesh and Sanctifying Spirit," in *Wesleyan Theological Journal* 49, no. 1 (2014): 175-85.

The contributors have been Bill's teachers, or teaching colleagues, one of his students, or a fellow student during school. Each writer is a friend who has formed Bill's life, academically and spiritually. The mutuality of reciprocal love and life exchange represented in the history of these friendships, is itself a manifestation of triune holy love. You will read about them and their relationship to Bill at the beginning of their chapters.

Dr. Dennis F. Kinlaw, is now at home in the bosom of the Trinity. His brilliant mind and self-offering heart of love and intimate friendship has been significant to Bill's life and ministry. The ways that Bill thinks and lives in some manner, were nurtured out of the richness of Kinlaw's investment in him. His essay is first, because of that long influence. It is contributed via Cricket Albertson.

The appendix contains short contributions of personal tribute offered by others. I received harsh reprimand from each of them for limiting their word count.

Biography

M. William Ury was raised in Taiwan, the son of United Methodist missionaries. He received a Bachelor of Arts degree in History from Asbury College in 1978. For the first year of his Master of Divinity degree, he studied at the Institute of Holy Land Studies on Mt. Zion in Jerusalem. He took every class they offered. During seminary, Dr. Dennis Kinlaw invited Bill to take a year off from the classroom and spend it traveling with him around the world as he taught. He fed Bill countless books and quizzed him on airplanes and in hotel rooms, training him how to think in trinitarian personal categories.

After earning a Master of Divinity degree at Asbury Theological Seminary in 1983, Bill went on to study theology at Drew University in Madison, New Jersey. Tom Oden, Jim Paine, Bard Thompson, and others were major influences on his love for the Church Fathers and historical theology. He received his Master of Philosophy degree in 1986 and Doctor of Philosophy degree in 1991. Personal friendships with Oden and Paine set the trajectory for Bill's academic life.

Bill never studied on the Sabbath all the years he was in graduate school. Even when slightly mocked for this by his fellow students because he would be facing Bard Thompson in tutorial on Monday, Bill rested from his work. I believe this bore fruit. Only because I was present at his dissertation defense, his major advisor told me, "Bill received highest distinctions on both his written dissertation and his defense. His is one of the best dissertations ever produced by this university." I know if Dr. Bull hadn't told me that personally, I still would not know it, because Bill would never have told me to this day.

While in New Jersey, Bill and Diane served as associate pastors in a Chinese-American United Methodist Church in Chinatown, New York City. After graduate work he began to teach Systematic and Historical Theology at Wesley Biblical Seminary (WBS) where he had the privilege of serving for nearly twenty-four years. He continues at WBS serving as Professor Emeritus and adjunct in the Doctor of Ministry program. Bill taught Sunday school weekly for twenty years at Christ United Methodist Church in Jackson, Mississippi. Throughout his adult life, weekly discipleship groups of seminary students and laymen continuously met with him for accountability and the means of grace.

Bill continues to serve as an evangelist at camp meetings and local churches, and as seminar leader, as he has for forty years. Bill always took at least one of his children — sometimes all of them at once — with him whenever he traveled to speak anywhere, even if they were still in diapers, and unaccompanied by their mother. This was a huge source of joy for both the children and for Bill. Since 1997 Bill has served as the preacher on a nationwide program under the auspices of American Family Radio, entitled "The Hour of Holiness." His podcast is of the same name with hundreds of regular listeners. For five years, the Urys pastored Elizabeth City

Evangelical Methodist Church in North Carolina. At present Bill and Diane serve as the National Ambassadors for Holiness with The Salvation Army, teaching Wesleyan holiness theology throughout the denomination, both nationally and internationally.

Beyond writing articles on biblical and theological themes, Bill has written *Trinitarian Personhood: Investigating the Implications of a Relational Definition*, and *The Bearer: Forgiveness from the Heart*. Along with five workbooks on discipleship, he co-authored *In His Image* with Dr. Allan Coppedge. Bill has been the guest lecturer at several institutions, including Trinity Evangelical Divinity School, Asbury University, and Wesley Biblical Seminary. He presents implications of Trinitarian Personhood on issues such as creation and anthropology.

Bill and Diane have been married since 1984 and have enjoyed a lifetime of ministry together. They have four married children and eight grandchildren — so far. In order to be near their family, their home is in Raleigh, North Carolina.

CHAPTER ONE

Holy Love and Personhood

Dennis F. Kinlaw
(via Cricket Albertson)

Tribute

I had the beautiful privilege of observing the long-lasting friendship between my grandfather, Dennis Kinlaw and Bill Ury. From student, to traveling companion, to theological dialogue partner, Bill engaged Dr. Kinlaw with a persistence and intensity that brought immense joy to the heart of my grandfather. Their conversations opened doors of spiritual and theological possibility for themselves and for those of us who happened to be listening. Both "Papa" and Bill shared a passionate interest in personhood, coming out of their own deep love of the Lord Jesus and a determined hunger to understand and articulate the depths of His divine and human nature. They shared a common desire to understand, explore, and share the beauty of the Wesleyan Trinitarian message, and when they came together their love for Christ deepened and their commitment to share God's holy love increased. The friendship between the two of them grew from that of a teacher to student to one of kindred spirits in Christian witness, deepening faith, and intellectual journey. Like "iron sharpening iron," their conversations strengthened and sharpened the faith and theological insight of many of us who follow in their footsteps.

Essay

One of the more difficult subjects to grasp in our search to understand the biblical teaching on the triune character of God lies in the development of the concept of personhood. The understanding of personhood grew out of conversations concerning the identity of Jesus and His relatedness to the Father. One of the greatest problems for the Christian Church in the development of the doctrine of the Trinity was that of vocabulary. Precision in definition became the test of orthodoxy. Intuitively as well as intellectually the Fathers realized that everything depended upon linguistic accuracy in the matter of triune identity. They were dealing with the very nature of the deity. A misrepresentation in terminology could leave the Church worshipping a god who did not really exist. They realized that this was a life-or-death question, and so the arguments concerning the nature of Jesus became sharp on occasion.

The early Christians scoured the words of Jesus about His relationship to the Father to determine, not what God does, but who He is in His inner being, in His very essence. A radically new concept of God was the result. The New Testament picture of the inner life of God is not one of power, or infinity, or omniscience. These are attributes that the church came to apply to God, and rightly so. However, three persons living one life in holy love, self-giving and self-sacrificing, became the message of the early Christian Church.

The problem of the otherness within the oneness now took center stage. The supreme characteristic of the life of God is an other-orientedness that could never exist if God were simply the great sovereign monad. Love becomes, not merely something that God does, but who He is in His very essence. It is significant that it is the Johannine literature which makes most plain the inner relations within the Godhead. It is this which gives us the ultimate definition of God as holy love. This means now that the supreme goodness of God is not seen in God's acts of love to us, but God who is love invites us into that very life of love which is His inner self. The call to love must be understood in the light of the picture which Jesus gives of how the Father and the Son and the Spirit relate to each other. It is a relationship of an other-oriented, self-sacrificial giving of oneself to the others. What we see in the inner life of God is the ultimate ground of all existence from which everything comes and from which everything draws its sustenance.

This concept of God finally enabled the church to make sense of the words of Jesus about His relationship to the Father. Jesus was very clear that He knew His life was not in Himself, that it came from another, that it came from the Father: "For as the Father has life in himself, so he had granted the Son to have life in himself" (John 5:26). Often through the centuries there has been a tendency to see this as an expression of Jesus in His humanity. The context, though, does not permit this. It is the second person of the Triune

Godhead who acknowledges that He, the Son, receives His life as a gift from the Father. He is after all the only begotten Son of the Father (John 1:14, 18, 3:16, 18; I John 4:9) and that "begottenness" is an eternal relationship. His umbilical cord has still not been cut, for He eternally draws His life from the Father.

The first great problem for the early Church in understanding Jesus was to find language to save the oneness of God without forfeiture of Christ. They did this by pouring new meaning into the Greek concept of *being* so that it could be used to speak of a God who transcended His own creation and who was holy. Then it could be used to speak of the oneness of God. The Christian God is one Being, and Jesus, God's Son, shared with the Father that Being. This enabled them to maintain Christ's deity. But how were they to save the distinctions in God that would keep the otherness of the Father, the Son, and the Spirit from being dissolved into a monadic univocity in which their individuality would be lost? They found the answer to that problem in the term *person*.

Originally the word *persona* (the Latin equivalent of the Greek *prosopon*) meant simply *face*. So, the first Christians said that in Jesus they had seen the very face of God. What Moses had been denied (Exodus 33), they, through Christ, had been permitted to see. They had met face-to-face with God. The words *persona* and *prosopon* developed a second meaning. They came to be used of the mask which actors would wear in a dramatic play to indicate the role that an actor was playing. This seemed an appropriate word to be used of Jesus, for it was obvious to the early Church that Jesus played a role that only God could perform. Who beside God can forgive sins? Furthermore, in a drama an actor comes to reflect the character of the person whom he represents on stage. So, the term begins to speak of the quality and the significance of the one whose role the actor plays. The symbol begins to speak of the reality represented by that symbol.

The early Church saw in Jesus a revelation of God in one who played a part that only God could play, and who did it in such a way that the very character of God was revealed to them. It was not a long jump for them to conclude that in Jesus they had seen God in human flesh, that He really did merit the name Immanuel, "God with us." Jesus for them was a person, a divine person, God's very Son.

It did not come immediately, and it is not our place here to develop that story, but it was inevitable that the same logic had to be applied to the Holy Spirit who filled the church at Pentecost. The result was a faith that proclaims that God is one Being, but within that Being are three persons: the Father, the Son, and the Spirit. One God in three persons and three persons in one Being became the key. But was a person, a divine person, more than a face, a role, and a character? What does it mean to be a person?

As the church wrestled with the question of Jesus and His identity as a person, it came to feel that a person is one with an individual and unique consciousness of himself or herself as oneself. This was obvious in the speeches of Jesus in the Gospels where He spoke of His relationship to His Father. He knew that He was not the Father and that the Father was not the Son. The Son's sonship was a gift to Him from His Father. Therefore, He was intimately related in His inner being to the Father, but He was not the Father. In the same way the Father was not the Son, never had been and never would be. Each had a distinct identity, and the character of that identity was determined by their relationship with each other. Each had His own name. Each was a person, uniquely distinct from all other persons. That same distinctness that they saw in Jesus they slowly began to recognize in the Spirit. God is one being in three persons.

A second characteristic of a person is that persons never come alone. They always come in webs of relationships. Those relationships do not remove their individual uniqueness, but they have a determinative effect upon the person's being. Jesus could not think of Himself apart from His sonship to the Father. That was the key factor in letting Him know who He was. The distinctness was as real as the relationship, but the relationship was as real as the distinctness. Like the obverse and the reverse of a coin, both are essential to the nature of the being. Thus, the early Church recognized a triadic distinction in the Trinity where the separateness of the persons protected the identity of the persons, but it did it in such a way that their oneness was not lost either. God is one Being in three persons and three persons in one Being.

The third conclusion which the early Church drew about God was that the character of the relationship of the three persons in the Godhead was a reciprocal relationship. It was one of a mutual giving and receiving. They were distinct from each other but not independent of each other. The giving and receiving was not that of giving and receiving gifts, but life. The Father has life in Himself, and He gives His life to the Son. The Son draws His life from the Father. The Spirit likewise draws His life from the Father and the Son. The technical terminology is that He proceeds from the Father and the Son. But He does not live that life independently. His chief purpose is to glorify the Father and the Son. Thus, the character of the being of God has a certain "other-orientedness, a self-giving, self-sacrificing being for others. John says it simply with His twice repeated affirmation, "God is love." Love is not first something God does. It is who He is. It is possible because of the triune personhood where the three persons of the Godhead live together in a oneness of love. So, to be a person is to find one's life from, for, and in another.

The fourth characteristic that marked a person for these early Christians is freedom. There is no necessity in God. There is nothing external or internal to God that forces Him. The other-orientedness that is so much a part of His essential being is not compelled. He is love. That is His nature, and He chooses to be Himself. He did not create the world because of any necessity. He needed nothing beyond Himself to complete Himself. He chose in His freedom to create an object for His love. He did not give His Son to the world for any other reason than love. The fact that each person in the Trinity draws His life from the others in the Trinity does not affect this freedom. The receiving only means that they have that which they can freely give. That means that the love within God is not compelled. It is chosen. God's act reflected in that text, "For God so loved the world that he gave" is simply an expression of that freedom.

The fifth characteristic of a person is that the fulfillment of personhood is never in the self. It is always in another, and the fulfilling comes only in self-giving love which is free to sacrifice itself for another. That means that the key to one's being as a person is never within oneself. It is never found by turning within. It is only found by turning outside oneself. Thus, our completeness is never found in our individuality. Our individuality finds within itself a cry for another. The inner life of God is thus a transcendent communion of personal Being.

Human persons were created to be a part of that communion. Our turning away from God and into ourselves brought the original rupture in that communion. Now the Father has sent His Son to give Himself in sacrificial love to make it possible for human persons to enter again into that transcendent holy fellowship with the One who is the source and the fulfillment of life.

This understanding of human personhood runs head on into conflict with the modern view of individualistic human autonomy.

In the Christian view, each person has her own name and self-consciousness, yet each is found in a web of relationships that determines identity and fulfillment. Instead of being whole in oneself, a person is incomplete. In fact, if we had a perfect person, he or she would be incomplete. Even if we had a divine person, he would be incomplete, for a person is not complete in himself or herself. Thus, the eternal Son of God could say, "I can do nothing of myself."

Jeremiah understood this. In a priceless passage on the nature of God and the tendency of human persons to make an alternative to fill that gap in life, Jeremiah concludes, "I know, O Yahweh, that Adam's way is not in himself. It is not in the individual who walks to direct His steps." The reference to "Adam's way" is Jeremiah's way of including all of us without exception. A characteristic of the human person is that his "way" is not in himself. The expression "who walks" is a Semiticism for goal-orientedness. The prophet is concluding that the end for which we exist, collectively or individually, is not to be found in us. We are made for something, an Other, beyond ourselves.

No human being is self-originating. Every one of us began our existence inside the body of another person and the gift of life was the result of two other persons' decision. No human person is self-subsisting. At birth we begin to draw our life from our environment instead of from our mother. We cannot live from our own resources. Bread and water are essential. Sixteen times a minute our body, without any decision on our part, reaches out for oxygen. Our life is not in ourselves.

Nor is a human person self-explanatory. There is no such thing as a typical person for we come in two editions: male and female. If someone from a remote universe captured one of us, no manner of dissection would ever explain what we are. To be a male means to be incomplete just as to be female means to be incomplete. Our very bodies tell us that we are made for another and for another who is different from one's own self. A person alone is the picture of perfect sterility.

With this true, should it be too surprising to find that we are not self-fulfilling. Our fulfillment is supposed to be in another. As we said, persons come in webs of relationships. If the relationships are broken, the person suffers. Having come from the hand of God we are made for relationship with Him just as, having come from a love relationship between two humans, we need a relationship with one we call "mother" and another whom we call "father." To be deprived of either of these relationships is disastrous. To be deprived of the relationship with God is ultimate death. Persons never come alone, and loss of essential relationships is depersonalizing and dehumanizing.

For the Christian this view of human personhood is not surprising. We speak sometimes of a "God shaped vacuum" within us. We say that God made us for Himself and that we are incomplete without Him in our lives. God did not make us different from Himself so we would need Him; He made us like Himself. He made us in His own image and likeness, the very likeness of the Son. He made us as a person just as the Son is a person and as He is not complete in Himself, nor are we. Persons, divine or human, cannot live without relationships. The Bible places such an emphasis upon holy love. We are made for love, not a love that uses us for its own satisfaction but a love, a holy love, that finds its fulfillment in giving itself to and for another.

The early Church was conscious that God had made us in God's own image. They were aware that the image had been flawed by sin and that human persons are not what God intended them to be. The Church leaders came to feel that, in line with Paul's understanding of Christ as the second Adam as presented in 1 Corinthians 15, Jesus was God's new man, the beginning of the new creation, and that in Him we could see what a true human person was supposed to be. The church in subsequent centuries had difficulty in maintaining the insights found in those first centuries. The result was a limited understanding of humanity and humanity's possibilities. It also meant that the Church did not always see the fullness of what Christ died to do now for fallen men and women. If our understanding of the image of God is faulty, then it is inevitable that we will be wrong in our understanding of what Paul meant when he spoke of our being renewed in the image of the one who created us (Col 3:10). Only this kind of understanding of personhood can enable us to make sense of Paul's remarkable admonition to imitate God. We cannot imitate Him in His characteristics such an omnipotence, omniscience, or immutability. We are to be like Him in His essential nature which is holy love. We are imitating God and living in love as Christ loved us and gave Himself for us. In such self-giving, holy love, we become sweet smelling aroma to God just as Christ was. The purpose of the incarnation and the cross was to make this possible.

Dennis Kinlaw, former president of Asbury College (Wilmore, KY) graduated from Asbury College (1943) and Asbury Theological Seminary (1946). He received further training from Edinburgh and Princeton and then earned an M.A (1963) and Ph.D. (1967) from Brandeis University. He served as the first pastor of Loudonville Community Church in Loudonville, NY from 1952-1963. In 1963 he returned to Asbury Theological Seminary as a professor of Old Testament history, theology, and languages. His love and passion for students and academics led him to accept an invitation to serve as president of Asbury College. He served from 1968-1981 and then from 1986-1991. In 1983 he founded the Francis Asbury Society in Wilmore, KY to encourage the Wesleyan holiness world through publishing, evangelism, and revival. He served as an editor for Christianity Today *and chairman of the board for OMS International.*

CHAPTER TWO

Holy Love and Creation

Mark Bird

Tribute

In the Spring of 1994, I went to Jackson MS to attend Wesley Biblical Seminary for the semester. I remember my first evening in Dr. Ury's History of Christian Thought class. My head literally hurt by the end of the three-hour class time with so many new terms, so much information, so many powerful insights. Not a boring moment — a very stretching time. What a fountain to drink from that semester. The final exam was three or four essay questions that I had three hours to answer from memory. I remember that my handwritten product was sixteen pages. I learned more from that class than I had learned in any other class up to that point, or maybe ever. I had taken theology and Church history classes before, but it was Ury who opened up for me the world of classic Christianity. I understood what the Christian tradition really meant. I understood the importance of the creeds and the voice of the Church Fathers. Including other classes I took from Bill, I gained a vital and wonderful understanding of Wesleyan theology in the context of the whole Christian tradition.

Bill continues to mentor me, decades later. His breadth of theological knowledge and depth of humble godliness remain an inspiration to me. Whether I'm studying a biblical passage or a Christian writer, he's able to guide me to deeper spiritual insights, or to a perspective I wouldn't have come up with on my own. Besides the personal interaction, his popular Hour of Holiness broadcast has been a blessing to me, and I hope more and more people hear about it and listen. It's been a privilege for me to work together with Dr. Ury in higher education in recent years, and to contribute to this volume of essays in his honor.

Essay

Love first existed in the Trinity. The eternal love between the members of the Godhead was completely satisfying. God needed no one outside the Triune life for personal fulfillment.* Yet God created. Why? Because Creation is the overflow of Triune love.

In the book *Discovering the Character of God*, George McDonald described the nature of God's love and how it relates to His creation. McDonald said, "Love is the deepest depth, the essence of His

---

* This assertion is based on the historic doctrine of the self-sufficiency of God. He has no needs (Acts 17:24-25).

nature, at the root of all His being. Love is the heart and hand of His creation." Yes, God has the right to create and the power to create. "But it is out of love that He *does* create."[*]

This love, as self-giving goodness seeking the good of another, is a holy love. Holy love is the essence of God's moral character, and He created us to have a holy love relationship with Him. Bill Ury explained, "When that limitless love creates, the result is persons who are formed by that love for love. And the freedom to choose to return that love is foundational to human personhood."[†] Genuine love implies freedom.[‡]

Understanding God's moral character as essentially holy love should shape our view of how God brought everything into the world and how He even now relates to all His creation, including humanity. From that perspective, this essay defends the traditional Creation/Fall/Redemption/Restoration narrative of Scripture. I briefly critique the idea that God used billions of years of evolutionary processes, with all its suffering, deformities, disease, destruction, and extinction, to bring about a "very good" Creation. My focus is not on the age of the earth itself, but on the wholeness and goodness of God's creation work. I believe that when a holy, loving God created a "very good" world, it reflected His goodness in an originally idyllic (peaceful and pleasant) state.

---

[*] George McDonald, *Discovering the Character of God*, essays compiled by Michael Phillips (Bloomington, MN: Bethany House, 2000), 31 (italics original).

[†] Bill Ury, "Creation and Imaging the Holy One," Unpublished paper presented at the Chamberlain Holiness Lectures, Wesley Biblical Seminary, on Oct 8, 2019.

[‡] Love is always offered freely, or it is not truly love. God made us in His image with the genuine freedom to accept and extend love or to reject it. And the love of God is extended to all. I disagree with theological determinism for the same reason I do not believe disease, sickness, extreme pain, and deformities existed before the Fall. These ideas appear to be inconsistent with the holy, loving character of God.

Dogma

Those of us who had the privilege of having Bill Ury as a seminary professor likely remember his emphasis on dogma. The term "dogma" can be used to refer to more than what the Church considers to be essential doctrine; the concept can also be personalized. Ury defined dogma as "the basic, or essential, view of reality that informs (has explanatory power for) every other aspect of life — ontology, epistemology, beliefs, and ethics." One's personal dogma is his set of overarching beliefs, or presuppositions, that serve as the interpretive grid through which he understands all other things.[*]

The holy love of God is part of my interpretative grid. How I understand Creation is shaped by my appreciation of the holy, compassionate character of God as revealed in Scripture.

I'm also convinced that this holy God inspired the Bible in such a way that it is harmonious, authoritative, and inerrant. I understand the words of each Bible writer as also the very words of God.[†] This high view of Scripture explains my perspective on science. I choose to hold the conclusions of the scientific community subordinate to my best understanding of Scripture. If the Bible really teaches that out of love, God originally made everything flawless and whole, then we have warrant to believe that even if most scientists believe otherwise.[‡]

---

[*] This is not to say that we create our own truth. Truth is objective. Truth is not truth unless it corresponds to reality. My point is that our fundamental beliefs or convictions color the way we see reality. If our fundamental beliefs are wrong, we are likely to misconstrue many other things.

[†] The syllogism that I use to argue for inerrancy is: Premise A: Every utterance of God is perfect and thus free from error. Premise B: All the truth claims of the Bible writers are the utterances of God. Conclusion: All the truth claims of the Bible writers are free from error.

[‡] Theologian Hans Madueme argues this in "All Truth is God's Truth: A Defense of Dogmatic Creationism," a paper presented at the Center for Pastor Theologians, Oak Park, IL., November 2017. He said that it is rational for us to believe in a recent Creation, even if

Origin of Species According to the Bible

To set the context for our case that God did not use millions of years of suffering and death to produce a "very good" creation, let's review the teachings about origins in the first chapters of Genesis.[*] There is no literary reason to view these chapters as anything other than historical narrative.[†] Genesis gives a factual and straightforward account of how it all began.

At the beginning of time, God (a timeless, incorporeal, and self-existing being) created the heavens and the earth (1:1) out of nothing, simply with an act of His will and by His Word. Initially, this planet was uninhabited and uninhabitable, but the Spirit of the eternal Creator hovered over the waters that covered the earth

---

contradicted by the international scientific community, because of our absolute confidence in the author of Scripture.

* Bill Ury said, "I believed, but now I am convinced, that without Genesis 1-2 we would be lost theologically. There would be no clear beginning of our reason for existence. Origin and purpose are inseparable. In my reading I have come across this important question at least twice, 'What are human beings for?' These chapters are the foundation of the only comprehensive answer to that startling realization. I can guarantee you that you will use the ideas found in Gen 1 and 2 for every issue touching humanity in our day. It must be a priority if you care about ethics, gender identity, sexuality, AI, robotics. I would add if you want to share the gospel in this age you must be fluent in these initial paragraphs of Scripture." (Ury, "Creation and Imaging the Holy One," 2019).

† Some say "exalted" prose narrative, but it is certainly not poetry. There is no Hebrew parallelism. The chapters were considered historical by Jesus and the Apostles. There are at least 25 NT passages that refer to Genesis 1-11 and "all 25 take the account literally." Todd Beall, "Contemporary Hermeneutical Approaches to Genesis 1-11," in *Coming to Grips with Genesis* (Green Forest, AR: New Leaf Publications), 146. In his essay, "Theistic Evolution Undermines Twelve Creation Events and Several Crucial Christian Doctrines," Wayne Grudem gives several reasons that Genesis 1-3 must be considered historical. He quotes James Hoffmeier, professor of OT and Near Eastern Archaeology at TEDS, who said, "Genealogical texts in the ancient Near East, by their very nature, are treated seriously by scholars and not cavalierly dismissed as made-up or fictitious, even if such lists are truncated or selected.... The 'family history' structuring [of Genesis] indicates that the narratives should be understood as historical, focusing on the origins of Israel back to Adam and Eve, the first human couple and parents of all humanity." J.P. Moreland, Stephen Meyer, Christopher Shaw, and Wayne Grudem, *Theistic Evolution: A Scientific, Philosophical, and Theological Critique* (Wheaton, IL: Crossway Books, 2017), 796.

(1:2-3). Day One continued with God creating a temporary light source so that the cycle of dark and light on the earth would begin that first day (1:4-5).*

On Day Two, God separated the waters above and below the expanse (1:6-8). On Day Three, God made the dry land, gathering the water into seas, and He also spoke into existence fruit-bearing trees and other vegetation that would grow on the newly dried earth (1:9-13). He made each plant and tree "according to its kind" (1:12), implying that one kind didn't evolve from or into another kind.

On Day Four, God spoke the sun and the moon into existence. These would give light to the Earth, one during the day and one during the night (1:14-19). Also, on Day Four, He made the stars, somehow making their light appear on the Earth as He "stretched out the heavens" (Isaiah 45:12), in possibly a literal sense.† Notice that God created the plants before He created the sun.

On Day Five, God spoke into existence sea creatures and birds. He made each of these "according to its kind," and He declared that they were to reproduce, according to their kind (1:20-23).

On Day Six, God made land creatures according to their kind (1:24-25). He also made man and woman in His image (1:26-27). According to Genesis 2:7, God made man from dust, adding the divine breath, and Adam became a living being. God did not take a

---

* The text doesn't say the light was temporary, but this is an assumption based on the fact that there isn't a separate light that illumines the earth now besides the sun and the moon. Maybe the original disembodied light was later incorporated into the light of the sun.
† Some creationist astrophysicists have suggested that Einstein's general theory of relativity helps us understand how light could pass quickly through the warp of our time-space universe. Explaining how light from distant stars became visible from the earth in a relatively short time is one of the biggest challenges for creationists. Yet evolutionists have essentially the same problem. Astrophysicist Dr. Danny Faulkner explains the evolutionists' problem and various creationist distant starlight models at https://answersingenesis.org/astronomy/starlight/what-about-distant-starlight-models/. Of course, getting the light to the Earth in a day is not a problem for a miracle-working God, even if we don't know how to explain it.

pre-existing living being and turn it into the first man.* Once Adam named the animals, he recognized he was the only human (2:20). So, God put him to sleep, performed the first surgery, and made a woman from Adam's rib. Like Adam, Eve didn't have human parents.†

All theories of common descent are incompatible with the teaching of this passage. No other humans existed on the sixth day of creation.‡ As distinct creatures made in God's image, Adam and Eve began the human race.

Image of God in Man

The context of God's making man in His image (1:26-27) is the scene in which He had just made all kinds of land animals (1:24-25). In this passage, God shows a definite contrast between the nature of animals and humans. Man was created in God's likeness, designed for a special kind of relationship with Him and with each other, "made for mutual self-giving, reciprocal knowing, for communion."§ The ability to have freely chosen love relationships is a core aspect of the image of God in man. Animals do not have that capacity. Man having the freedom to choose relationships makes love genuine and sin possible.

---

* 'Living being' in verse 7 is a translation of the Hebrew *nephesh chayyah*. Sea creatures, birds and land animals are also called *nephesh chayyah* in Gen. 1:20-21, 24, 2:19, and 9:9-16. See OT professor William Barrick's discussion in his chapter in Terry Mortenson, ed., *Searching for Adam* (Green Forest, AR: New Leaf Publishing Group, 2016), 25-26.
† According to 1 Corinthians 11:8, Paul accepted this to be true too.
‡ Eve is called "the mother of all living" (Gen. 3:20) and Adam was "the first man" (1 Cor. 15:45).
§ Bill Ury, 2019.

Good God; Good Creation

Notice that God (*Elohim*) described His creative work as "good" (*tov*) six times in Genesis 1. The seventh time that He contemplated His creation, He declared that it was "*very* good" (*tov me'od*).* Elohim was pleased with what He had created, as an artist might be with his painting. It was flawless; everything had its place, and everything was in its place. It was of the highest quality. It was functioning the way He intended it to function. It was harmonious and beautiful. There was no suffering, no disease, no violence, no evil. It was perfect because He is perfect; it was good because He is good.†

In a lecture on the goodness of creation, Craig Bartholomew quoted Jewish scholar Edwin Good on God's declaration that His creation was *tov me'od*: "Elohim is seldom an exaggerator, but I think this is a remarkably understated sentence when you consider the extent of what Elohim has done in a very short time." Bartholomew added that the Hebrew word *tov* "carries with it the connotation of not

---

* Genesis 1:31. "Very good" (*tov me'od*) is the superlative of "good" (*tov*), found in verses 4, 10, 12, 18, 21, and 25. It may be that God made the "good" judgment about the moral excellence and beauty of the parts, and used the superlative to describe the whole. Also, Bill Ury notes that he called creation "very good" after He made man and woman (Systematic Theology class lectures).

† In response to the question as to whether God may have intentionally used *tov* (good) instead of *tamim* (perfect) to make room for imperfections such as animal death, British theologian Craig Bartholomew replied: "Once we've listened to the way that the Israelites would have read the creation narrative, then we can then ask, 'How does Genesis 1:1-2:3 address 21st century scientific questions?' That's my strategy. I don't know the answer to animal death; I'm just not sure Genesis is trying to address that. So then to argue that *tov* is deliberately used to create space for that; it sounds to me too much like letting 21st century questions set the agenda, and I'm reluctant to do that." He also said, "If the use of *tov* rather than *tamim* means that creation is less than good, then I think no, there is no significance in that." Craig Bartholomew, "The Goodness of Creation and Its Ethical Implications," a lecture given for the Creation Project at the Henry Center, Chicago, Ill., April 12, 2018, https://henrycenter.tiu.edu/resource/the-goodness-of-creation-and-its-ethical-implications/

merely general excellence or of moral excellence but also of beauty."*

God called His creation "very good" because it reflected His good character. Psalm 135:3 says that we should praise the Lord, for "the Lord is good; sing to his name, for it is pleasant!" (Or, "for he is beautiful!").† The goodness of God is associated with the pleasantness of His name, or the beauty of His character. Psalm 145 extols God for His holiness and love, connecting these attributes to His mercy over His creation:

> The Lord is gracious and merciful,
> slow to anger and abounding in steadfast love.
> The Lord is good to all,
> and his mercy is over all that he has made (8-9).
>
> The eyes of all look to you,
> and you give them their food in due season.
> You open your hand;
> you satisfy the desire of every living thing.
> The Lord is righteous in all his ways
> and kind in all his works (16-17).

God called His Creation "very good" because it corresponded to His faithful, loving, beautiful character. We can assume that the original Creation was pleasant to behold; it was beautiful, and there was nothing hurtful or destructive in it.‡

---

* Craig Bartholomew, "The Goodness of Creation and Its Ethical Implications." In this lecture, Bartholomew also pointed out that part of the goodness of Creation is its openness towards a *telos*. Goodness doesn't mean it is the final product. Bartholomew's point here is consistent with an idyllic Creation since development doesn't necessarily entail suffering and death.

† ESV gives that alternate translation of the Hebrew word, *nā'îm*, a word translated sometimes in other passages as: "sweet," or "lovely."

‡ I'm using the language of Isaiah 65:25 here. Isaiah is describing a kingdom to come but this may represent a restoration of what was lost from the original creation: 'The wolf

Two Pictures of a "Good" God

Not everyone understands God's goodness in the same way. Thane Ury stated that "to say that creation is now in a fallen state due to sin (traditionalist view), as opposed to saying the present creation is exactly the way that an all-loving, all-powerful God intended it from the beginning (accommodationist view), is to paint two conflicting pictures of a good God."* Which picture is accurate?

In a debate with William Lane Craig, atheist Christopher Hitchens acknowledged that many Christians now accept macroevolution. He then mocked Christians for thinking that God would use evolution to bring us into the world. Unlike many Christians, this atheist saw the inconsistency between a loving God and such a cruel, wasteful process:

> And you too are quite free to believe that a sentient creator deliberately, consciously put himself or herself or itself to the trouble of going through huge epochs of birth and death of species over eons of time, over the course of which 99.9% of all species have become extinct, as we nearly did as a species ourselves. You have to be able to imagine that all this mass extinction and death and randomness is the will of a being. And all of this should happen so that one very imperfect race of evolved primates should have the opportunity to become Christians — the tremendous wastefulness of it, the tremendous cruelty of it, the tremendous caprice

---

and the lamb shall graze together; the lion shall eat straw like the ox, and dust shall be the serpent's food. They shall not hurt or destroy in all my holy mountain,' says the Lord."
* Thane Ury, "Luther, Calvin, and Wesley on the Genesis of Natural Evil: Recovering Lost Rubrics for Defending a Very Good Creation," in *Coming to Grips with Genesis*, ed. Terry Mortenson and Thane Ury (**Green Forest, AR:** New Leaf Publishing Group, 2008), 417.

of it, the tremendous tinkering and incompetence of it, never mind, at least we're here and we can be people of faith. It doesn't work for me.*

I agree with Hitchens here. This picture seems inconsistent with a holy, loving God, who told us to humanely care for our own animals.† I believe the accurate picture of a good God is One who made everything work beautifully together in the beginning. It is sin that brought death, disease, and suffering into the world.

The Fall and Natural Evil

The Fall wreaked havoc on Creation. In Genesis 3, we find that animals and the ground were cursed (resulting in thorns) *after* Adam's sin (Gen. 3:14-19).‡ We now experience severe pain, disease, and calamity because of moral evil. Natural evil is the consequence of moral evil. And it came *after* moral evil was introduced into the world.

The most popular and challenging objection to Christianity is the problem of evil: Why would an all-powerful and all-good God allow sin and suffering into the world? The theologians with the best

---

* Transcribed from the "Does God Exist?" debate between Christopher Hitchens and William Lane Craig at Biola University, April 4, 2009, https://www.youtube.com/watch?v=0tYm41hb48o, 38:35-41:15. I left out words that were not directly relevant to the point I am making with this quote.
† Proverbs 12:10. Deuteronomy 22:6-7. God cares for His creatures (Ps. 104:14-16 and 27-28; Matthew 6:26-28). Without ignoring the qualitative differences between consciousness in animals and humans, we should acknowledge the modern scientific research that has shown that many animals experience a wide range of emotions. This is an ethical problem for those who believe in animal death before the Fall.
‡ One example of cursed-liked conditions in the fossil record is evidence of cancer in dinosaur fossils. Because the diseases look the same, medical schools are beginning to have their students study cancer in dinosaur bones. See Heather Whipps, "Dinosaur Tumor Studied for Human Cancer Clues," April 3, 2006, www.livescience.com/4013-dinosaur-tumor-studied-human-cancer-clues.html.

response to this question — the best theodicy — are those who can use both the freewill defense and the response that natural evil came both *because* and *after* the Fall. Suffering came into the world when man abused his freedom by disobeying God's single command. The freewill defense says that since man could have chosen differently, God is not ultimately responsible for evil — man is. Theologians who reject libertarian freedom must look elsewhere for theodicies, and they come up short.* Those who say the earth went through a long process of suffering, disease, and extinction before the first humans also give an inadequate defense of God's character.

Restoration Coming

According to Romans 8:20-21, all Creation is groaning in bondage to corruption, but it also anticipates the day it will be set free from the curse. Someday, there will be a new heaven and a new earth (Revelation 21-22). The earth will have perfect conditions again. Isaiah 11:6-9 indicates that there will come a day when natural predators live at peace with their former prey. This suggests that non-violence was the original state, even among animals. Genesis 1:29-30 teaches that man and the animals were all originally vegetarian.

---

* John S. Feinberg was my seminary Apologetics teacher. He told us in class that if we were Arminian, we had a theodicy that worked in our system — it was the freewill defense. But he told us that since he was a Calvinist, the freewill defense would not work for him. He had us read his book *Many Faces of Evil* (Grand Rapids: Zondervan, 1994), in which he developed a different theodicy, which I considered inadequate.

Historical Support for an Original Idyllic State and the Global Flood

The view of Creation held by the Church Fathers is contrary to macroevolution and pre-Adamic natural evil. Church historian Gregg Allison surveyed the first few centuries of the Church's doctrine of Creation and identified four themes that stood out:

There is only one God who alone is eternal, self-sufficient, omnipotent, wise, and sovereign.

1. This God created the universe and everything in it out of nothing.

2. Divine creation took place in six literal days in the not-too-distant past.*

3. The notion of an undirected process — a random collision of already existing elements — fortuitously resulting in the origin and development of the vast diversity of living beings currently in existence was strongly denounced and considered absurd.†

---

* This point was, however, never put into creedal confession. (Gregg Allison, "Theistic Evolution is Incompatible with Historical Christian Doctrine" in *Theistic Evolution*, 930). Augustine is an exception to the belief in a literal 6-day creation since he thought that God created the world in an instant. However, he rejected evolution (there was such a notion among the ancient Greeks and others) and believed in an originally good Creation. In regard to Genesis 1:31, he said, "Was it not obviously meant to be understood that there was no other cause of the world's creation than that good creatures should be made by a good God? In this creation, had no one sinned, the world would have been filled and beautified with natures good without exception." The City of God, 11.23.

† In his *Historical Theology*, Gregg Allison points out, "Although it is often thought that evolution did not present a challenge to the church until Charles Darwin's theory, such is not the case. The early church had to confront ancient philosophies that resembled modern evolutionary theories in some ways." Gregg R. Allison, *Historical Theology* (Grand Rapids, MI: Zondervan, 2011), 256. Chapter 12 of *Historical Theology* is a great resource for learning the Church's historic doctrine of divine creation, which remained relatively stable for 1800 years.

This was the doctrine of creation that the
early Christians embraced and defended. It was
enshrined in the first article of one of its earliest
and most widely influential creeds, popularly
known as the Nicene Creed: "maker of heaven
and earth, and of all things visible and invisible.[*]

The Church Fathers also affirmed a global Flood of judgment
that covered the whole earth.[†] One of these Church Fathers,
Augustine, argued in *The City of God* for the reasonableness of the
Flood rising fifteen cubits above the highest mountains.[‡] And while
Augustine thought that Creation was instantaneous, he did believe
in a fairly recent Creation and warned against accepting the view
that the world was old.[§]

Before the development of modern geology, the majority view
in the Church was that Creation was recent, the Flood was global,
and that natural evil was the result of God's curse at the Fall.[¶] The
Reformers and Post-Reformers certainly affirmed these statements.
For example, John Calvin asked: "Whence comes the cruelty of
brutes, which prompts the stronger to seize and rend and devour with
dreadful violence the weaker animals?" He asserted that if "the stain of
sin had not polluted the world, no animal would have been addicted
to prey on blood, but the fruits of the earth would have sufficed for

---

[*] Allison, *Theistic Evolution*, 933-944.
[†] Hugh Owen et al., *Foundations Restored: A Catholic Perspective on Origins*, (Mt. Jackson, VA: Kolbe Center for the Study of Creation, 2020).
[‡] "But they who contend that these things never happened, but are only figures setting forth other things, in the first place suppose that there could not be a flood so great that the water should rise fifteen cubits above the highest mountains." *The City of God*, 15.17. Augustine also affirmed a global Flood in *The City of God*, 12.11.
[§] Allison, *Historical Theology*, 259.
[¶] Thane Ury, *Coming to Grips with Genesis*, 402.

all.[*]

John Wesley also believed in a flawless original Creation. He said that God made it "unspeakably better than it is at present....without blemish. He made no death in the animal creation, neither....pain."[†] Wesley added that "the scriptural account of *natural*, flowing from *moral* evil, will easily and perfectly solve" questions like, "How can the invisible things of God be seen from such a ruined creation?"[‡] We understand from Scripture that man's sin brought upon the world a curse that affects everyone and everything. Yet the world is still beautiful in many respects. Though God's creation is damaged, we can still marvel at His glorious handiwork.

The Biblical Flood and Science

The Bible teaches that God destroyed the entire world with a Flood because of the extreme wickedness of the human population (Genesis 6:6, 11). Yet the holy God who was about to destroy the world had identified a righteous man "who found grace in the eyes of the Lord" (6:8). Therefore, God spared Noah and his family and thus preserved the human race — out of love.[§]

Is there any evidence that this worldwide catastrophe really

---

[*] John Calvin, *Commentary on Isaiah*, trans. William Pringle (Grand Rapids, MI: Eerdmans, 1948), 216.

[†] *The Works of the Rev. John Wesley* (London: Thomas Cordeux, 1812), 9:141.

[‡] *The Works of the Rev. John Wesley*, 14:150 (italics original).

[§] The Bible teaches that the Flood was global: 1. The water covered all the mountains (Gen. 7:19-20). 2. The purpose of the ark was to save two of every kind of land animal and birds (Genesis 7:1-3) and the Flood blotted out all the land animals and birds not in the ark (Gen. 7:21-23). 3. Noah's family and the animals had to stay on the ark for months after it stopped raining (Gen. 8:1-18). 4. The fountains of the deep were broken up and there was non-stop global rain (Gen. 7:11). This points to the catastrophic nature of the Flood. 5. The Apostle Peter refers to Noah's Flood as global and catastrophic (2 Peter 3:3-6, cf., 1 Peter 3:20 and 2 Peter 2:4-9).

happened? Several years ago, I went on a group trip through the Grand Canyon, rafting down the Colorado River. Accompanied by and instructed by young-earth geologist Andrew Snelling, we examined the rock layers and some of the fossils in those layers, as Dr. Snelling explained them in light of the Noachian Flood. My big takeaway from the trip was that though dating methods produce a great variety of results regarding the age of the rocks (because of the different assumptions that go into the various methods), there is no compelling reason for rejecting a plain reading of Genesis 1-11, at least on geological grounds. Instead, a good case could be made for a global, catastrophic Flood.[*]

Recent comprehensive apologetics books make little, if any, reference to Noah's Flood.[†] But Noah's flood is essential for understanding Earth history and our origins, and it should not be ignored. Since the Bible teaches that Noah's Flood was global and catastrophic, we should pay attention to the scientific evidence presented by Flood geologists.[‡] If the Flood is responsible for most of the geological record of rock layers and fossils, then there is no

---

[*] Andrew Snelling published a 2-volume, 1100-page book called *Earth's Catastrophic Past* (Dallas, TX: Institute for Creation Research, 2009). It has about 100 pages of biblical arguments and the rest consists of in-depth geological arguments and evidence, including on radiometric dating, written at a level that non-geologists can understand. A short non-technical, well-illustrated introduction to the geological evidence is John Morris, *The Young Earth* (Green Forest, AR: Master Books, 2007).

[†] For example, I found no reference to the Flood in Douglas Groothius's *Christian Apologetics: A Comprehensive Case for Biblical Faith* (Downer's Grove, IL: InterVarsity Press, 2011).

[‡] Here are some of the scientific reasons to believe in a global, catastrophic Flood: 1. There are fossils of sea creatures in rock layers high above sea level over all the continents. 2. Extensive fossil graveyards show that plants and animals were buried rapidly by massive sediment. 3. Rock layers have been traced all the way across continents, and their physical features indicate that the sediment creating those layers was deposited rapidly. 4. Little to no erosion between layers, which means they were laid down continuously upon one another. 5. Rock layers are bent without being fractured. This shows that they were rapidly deposited and folded while still wet and pliable. For more evidence of a global flood visit: https://www.icr.org/article/why-christians-should-believe-global-flood.

good reason to believe that these layers represent millions of years of death, disease, and extinction.*

Conclusion

God brought the world into existence out of the overflow of His eternal, Triune love. Humans are the pinnacle of His creation, made for a special love relationship with God. The world where the first humans were placed was perfect, beautiful, and harmonious. But human sin brought suffering, death, disease, deformity, and destruction into the world. Because of the wickedness of man, God brought a Flood upon the earth to destroy all animal and human life except for what He preserved on the ark. The Flood account highlights both the holiness and love of God.

Through divine revelation (the written Scriptures), we can understand why creation is no longer as harmonious as it once was. The once-perfect creation, made by the loving hand of the holy Creator, became flawed because of sin and God's holy curse. The damaged Creation now anticipates the day of complete redemption, when God makes all things new. In the meantime, God is calling all of us to Himself, restoring us by grace into the holy, love relationship He has from the beginning longed to have with His human creatures.

Dr. Mark Bird graduated from Wesley Biblical Seminary in 1996 with an M.A. in Theology. He earned a D. Min. from Grace Theological Seminary in

---

* This article by Terry Mortenson (PhD, history of geology) contains important information about the Flood: https://answersingenesis.org/the-flood/global/biblical-necessity-global-flood/.

2000. Mark is Professor of Theology at God's Bible School and College, where he has been a faculty member since 1997. He teaches courses such as Systematic Theology and Apologetics on both the undergraduate and graduate level. He has authored two books: How Can You Be Sure?, *a theological work on the subject of grace and salvation, and* Defending Your Faith, *which makes a case for the validity of Christianity. Mark is a member of the Evangelical Theological Society and the moderator of The Cincinnati Philosophy Meet Up Group, in which he holds discussions with atheists and agnostics. He is married to Dr. Kristin Bird, an educational consultant for Christian Schools. They have three daughters, Karissa, Megan, and Karina.*

CHAPTER THREE

Holy Love and Human Nature

Thomas H. McCall

Tribute

I went to seminary without any particular interest in theology. I knew very little about the doctrinal heritage of the Christian Faith and perhaps cared even less. I didn't reject orthodox Christology or the doctrine of the Trinity, but neither had I thought much about such doctrines and didn't consider them to be all that important for Christian life and ministry. And then I walked into my first theology class, and it is no exaggeration to say that my life changed. The lecturer was a brilliant young scholar named Bill Ury. He introduced me to the riches of the Christian theological tradition. He taught me to do theology that is grounded in, and accountable to, Scriptural revelation. He modeled for me how to learn with respect and gratitude from the insights of patristic and medieval theologians. He showed me how to engage — with humility, gentleness, and respect — with the philosophical and social currents of our own late-modern culture. He gave me a vision of the truth, beauty, and goodness of the Triune God whose nature is holy love, and he encouraged me to share the glorious gospel of Christ. Learning from Bill in a classroom is wonderful but hearing him preach the gospel is even better. He is a gifted teacher, a passionate preacher, and even better person. I will always be grateful for him.

Introduction

Confusion — and indeed consternation — about what it means to be human is rampant in contemporary Western culture. There are competing accounts of what it means to be human. Are we fundamentally meat-sacks that are geared only for survival and reproduction? Are we merely lumps of molecules that are hardwired for what Patricia Churchland memorably referred to as "the Four F's: feeding, fleeing, fighting, and reproducing"?* Are we complex machines whose actions are fully determined by our genetic inheritance and environments? Are we infinitely plastic and thus sentenced to the unbearable task of creating our own identity? Are we autonomous individuals who are hopelessly adrift in our own subjectivity? What does it mean to be human?

Christian theology has much to say to these questions, and what it says is of great importance. For Christian theology tells

---

* Patricia J. Churchland, "Epistemology in the Age of Neuroscience," *Journal of Philosophy* (1987), 548.

us that we humans — not only in our moments of transcendent greatness but also in our moments of fumbling finitude, even in our moments of pitiful and repulsive depravity — are made by God in the very image and likeness of God, that we are known by God and called by God, that we are redeemed by God for nothing less than fellowship and communion with the Triune God whose very essence is holy love.

Indeed, human nature, as such, has an essential capacity for holy love. This natural capacity is grounded in the extravagant generosity of the divine will, which in turn is the expression of the nature of the Triune God who *is* holy love.

The Nature of Human Nature: A Closer Look

What do we mean when we refer to the nature of something? More precisely, what do we mean when we refer to "human nature?" Following important recent developments in metaphysics, which in many respects are based upon deeply traditional views, let us clarify what we mean. Human nature is what may be called a "kind essence," or "kind nature". It is to be distinguished from what is sometimes called an "individual essence," or for the medieval theologians, a *haecceity*. While an individual essence belongs to a distinct entity, say, Rover the Black Labrador or Smoky the Quarter Horse, the kind essence is what is shared by all members of that "kind," in these instances, dogs and horses. Roughly, we can think of it as the difference between some particular thing and the "kind of thing" that it is. A bit more precisely, a kind essence is the full set of properties that are individually necessary and jointly sufficient for membership in that particular kind. The properties are individually necessary; one must have all of them to be included. And the properties are jointly sufficient. If you have all of them, then you just are a member.* Rover has to have all the properties of caninity to count as a dog, and Smoky must have all the properties of equinity to properly count as a horse. But if Rover and Smoky have such properties, then Rover *is* a dog and Smoky *is* a horse.

The distinction between *essential* properties and *accidental* properties is also important. Essential properties are those that one *must have* to be included as a member of the kind essence, while accidental properties are those that one might have or might not have. Essential properties are thus necessary for membership, but accidental properties are only contingent. Thus, Rover must have the properties necessary to have the kind essence *caninity*, but other properties — such as being stub-tailed due to an unfortunate lawnmower accident or one-eared due to an even more unfortunate coyote attack — are accidental. Rover could not exist without being a dog, but surely Rover could exist with a long tail and two ears.

This explanation may seem overly philosophical and thus at some distance from meaningful theological statements, so let us return to theological anthropology and explore the relevance for our central theological affirmation. With these brief clarifications about what it means to say something about a nature, how should we understand the claim that capacity for holy love is part of human nature?

Of course, there are many properties or attributes of human nature. What makes humans distinct from, say, anteaters and apes, or elves and orcs, is complicated and includes many facets. But we need not sort out all complexities or offer a full list of those

---

* Such distinctions have been used in Christology by Thomas V. Morris, *The Logic of God Incarnate* (Ithaca: Cornell University Press, 1986).

properties to grasp the central theological point. We might, for the sake of summary, simply say that humans are those creatures that are *homo sapiens* and made in the *imago dei*. Thus, under these two headings (*homo sapiens* and *imago dei*) we could, theoretically at least, list the attributes or properties of the kind essence *humanity.** A combined list of these two categories would tell us what the kind essence humanity — *humankind* — is, and we would know that anyone who is human has all such properties. Such a list would not include the accidental properties often associated with humankind. It would include only those that are necessary and thus essential. To cite a well-known example, while the property *being born on earth* is a common human property, nonetheless it is an accidental property of humankind rather than an essential property. We would not, for instance, deny the humanity of someone born on a lunar colony, and to suggest otherwise is morally heinous.

We are now in position to spell out further the claim that capacity for how holy love is essential to human nature. If someone is human, then that person has the capacity for holy love. Such a capacity is not accidental, not something that might or might not come with being human. No one is — nor even could be — a human who may or may not ever have this capacity. To the contrary, it is a necessary element of what it means to be human. It is part of what it means to be made in the image of God, for God's own nature is holy love. It is not something which must be earned or gained, it is not something bestowed on some humans but not others. It is not accidental, and in no sense is it fortuitous

---

* I think that I first heard this way of summarizing the issue in a conference presentation by Garrett Deweese. But cf. William Lane Craig's inclusion of Neanderthals (and other primates) in the category of human, *In Quest of the Historical Adam* (Grand Rapids: William B. Eerdmans Publishing Co., 2020).

or capricious. To the contrary, it is nothing less than essential. To be human — more precisely, to be a human *person* — means to be created with this innate capacity for holy love. For to be human is to be made by God, known by God, loved by God.

Holy Love: A Brief Exposition

There is much more that could be said, of course, about natures and persons. But with this much in hand, let us turn our attention to another vitally important question. What can we say about *holy love*?

Following the Christian tradition, we can say the following with confidence.* First, to love someone is to desire the best for that person. It is to want that person to flourish. It is to long for the wholeness of that person. It is to desire that that person's gifts are exercised, that their desires are both purified and fulfilled. It is to want to see that person experience and relish their full *telos* and to find their proper fulfillment and home. Second, to love someone is to desire union with that person. What the proper account of union is, of course, will vary by relationship. The union of parents with their children is one thing; the union of siblings is another; the union of friendship yet another; and the union of lovers joined in marriage is another thing entirely. The various cases of union will involve different versions of volitional, affective, and even physical union. But the basic point remains the same: whatever exactly the proper account of union is in a given relationship, to love someone is to desire union with that person. Third, and closely related, to love someone is to find joy in that person. It is to be fundamentally

---

* See the explication by Eleonore Stump, "Love, by All Accounts," *Proceedings and Addresses of the American Philosophical Association* (2006), 25-43.

glad that the other exists. It is to delight in their achievements, to exult in their successes.

Correspondingly, it is to share their sorrows and enter their grief. To love someone is to cherish them, to find delight in their very being, to see beyond oneself and to transcend the bonds of self-centeredness.

What does it mean to say that love is *holy* love? What difference does it make to say that love is holy? While a full exploration of this massive, and massively important, question is beyond the scope of this essay, we can make some meaningful affirmations. When we talk about holiness in a properly biblical and theological sense, we refer to both *transcendence* and *purity.*[*] Thus to say that God is holy is to say that God is utterly transcendent. God is not part of the created order, and God does not have the limitations that characterize and sometimes frustrate creatures. God is not dependent upon anything or anyone in all Creation to be who or what God is. God does not owe His existence to anyone, and God does not depend upon anyone for His actualization or fulfillment. God is wholly *other,* and it is recognition of this sense that produces the famous *mysterium tremendum et fascinans.*[†] Accordingly, God is never the object of manipulation and is never subject to cosmic power plays. As holy, God is completely stable and trustworthy. To say that God is holy is also to affirm that God is *pure.* God's character is completely unblemished; it has no taint of anything other than perfect beauty and splendor. God is not merely good — although of course this is a gloriously true statement. No, God is

---

* See the illuminating discussion in John N. Oswalt, *Called To Be Holy: A Biblical Perspective* (Nappanee: Evangel Press, 1999).
† This phrase comes from the famous work of Rudolph Otto, on which see Mark C. Murphy, *Divine Holiness and Divine Action* (Oxford: Oxford University Press, 2021).

perfectly good and necessarily good. There is no possibility that God could be anything other than good. Indeed, it is not so much as possible that God is anything less than *perfectly good.*

To say that God is holy is to stand in awe before the effulgence of the radiant and numinous divine beauty, and when we affirm that God is holy, we mean that God's goodness is unsurpassably great. It is to say, with St. John, that "God is light, and in him there is no darkness at all" (1 John 1:5). When we say that God is love, we do not mean simply that "God so loved the world" (John 3:16), for, again with St. John, we affirm that "God *is* love" (1 John 4:8, 16). So, when we say that God is holy love, we mean that this love is the essence of the Triune God as the very life shared by Father, Son, and Holy Spirit, and we mean that this love that is essential to God is unblemished by any hint of self-centeredness and untarnished by even the possibility of sin. The only "otherness" of the intra-divine life is the delight and joy in the union and communion of the Father, Son, and Holy Spirit. When we speak of God's holy love, we are, then, left in wonder and awe. For we are speaking of the "supreme ontological predicate."[*]

When we turn attention back to theological anthropology, what are we saying when we affirm that human nature includes the capacity for holy love? What is meant by this audacious claim? It means that we are made for love. We are creatures of the Triune God whose essence is holy love, and we come "from" that love. Jacob Arminius expresses well the traditional theological conviction that God created human creatures to "know, love, and worship" their Creator, and "to live blessed with Him in eternity."[†] For not only is

---

[*] John D. Zizioulas, *Being As Communion: Studies in Personhood and the Church* (New York: St. Vladimir's Seminary Press, 1985), 46.
[†] Jacob Arminius, *disp priv* xxvi.10.

God "the best; that, He is the first and highest good and goodness itself," He is also "ready to communicate that good as far as it can be communicated," and God's "great liberality is matched by the treasures He possesses."[*]

We are made by the God who is "onto-relational," and we are made for relationships that are to be characterized by holy love.[†] These relationships are, to put it plainly, both "vertical" and "horizontal." We are made with capacity for loving relationships with the Triune Creator and with one another. Thus, we are made to know God, to desire the best for God, to desire union with God, and to find delight in God. And thus, we are also made to know one another, desire the best for one another, desire the proper relationship of union with one another, and find delight and joy in one another. We are made as creatures capable of *love*. As Marilyn McCord Adams says, "Material persons are no more made for solo action than divine persons essentially are," and "Autonomous ego management is not the ultimate goal of human development."[‡]

And, to be clear, the love for which we are made is a *holy* love. It is love that is transcendent, for we are capable of rising above our own narcissist tendencies and self-centered corruption so that we truly come to desire the best for the other and take delight in the flourishing of the other. And it is love that is pure, untainted by the evil that corrupts and ruins and destroys. This happens only by

---

[*] See Keith D. Stanglin and Thomas H. McCall, *Jacob Arminius: Theologian of Grace* (New York: Oxford University Press, 2012), 47.

[†] This is a common theme in the theology of Thomas F. Torrance. See Gary W. Deddo, "The Importance of the Personal in the Onto-relational Theology of Thomas F. Torrance," in Myk Habets, ed., *T & T Clark Handbook of Thomas F. Torrance* (New York: T & T Clark/ Bloomsbury, 2020), 143-161.

[‡] Marilyn McCord Adams, "Sanctifying Matter," in Andrew B. Torrance and Thomas H. McCall, eds., *Knowing Creation: Perspectives from Theology, Philosophy, and Science* (Grand Rapids: Zondervan Academic, 2018), 176.

grace, of course, for sinful creatures are always dependent upon the prevenient, regenerating, and sanctifying grace of the Holy Spirit. But it *does* happen, for the Holy Spirit *does* continue to work in the hearts and lives of God's children to bring them to complete wholeness and holiness. And it finally *will be* accomplished, for the promise of the Father is that He is faithful and will bring this process to completion in full sanctification and glorification (cf. 1 Thessalonians 5:23).

Reasons to Believe: A Sketch

To this point, I have offered a very concise overview of a distinctly theological vision of human nature: the capacity for holy love is essential to human nature. But to this point I have only offered a set of affirmations that sound like mere assertions. What reasons might there be think that this vision corresponds to divine and human to hold the view I have sketched?

First, it is plausible to think that those creatures made in the divine image and likeness — *human persons* — would, in ways appropriate to finite creatures, reflect the characteristics that are essential to the Creator. And, as I and others have argued elsewhere, the conviction that holy love is of the essence of God has both a profoundly biblical basis and extensive recognition and development within the broad and deep Christian tradition.* If God is not only holy and loving but indeed *is* holy love, then it is not at all a stretch to conclude that human persons are created with an innate capacity for holy love. We are made to know and love

---

* See, e.g., Thomas H. McCall, "What's Not To Love?" *International Journal of Systematic Theology,* forthcoming.

God and one another. Of course, there are important differences. For instance, God is infinite and creatures are finite; God is both necessarily existent and necessarily perfectly good while humans are contingent and therefore only contingently good; God *is* holy love by nature and humans have a capacity for holy love by nature. But even granting the very important differences, nonetheless, on the basis of the doctrine of the *imago dei,* we can affirm that human persons are made with a capacity to know and love God and others. Human nature, as such, includes a capacity for holy love.

Second, let us also consider what is referred to in Scripture as the "Great Commandments." Jesus clearly states the "first and greatest" commandment: "You shall *love* the Lord your God with all your heart, and with all your soul, and with all your mind" (Matthew 22:37). And He follows this by adding the "second" which is "like it" — "You shall *love* your neighbor as yourself" (Matt 22:39). It is scarcely conceivable that the perfectly good God would call and command human persons to do something that is impossible. To the contrary, we have every good reason to believe that the divine invitation, command, and promise is something that God wants and wills. Thus, it must be something that is genuinely possible, by divine enablement, for humans. And, if so, then the capacity for holy love is truly a possibility for humans.

There are, of course, important issues and questions to be considered further. Some might object that, in point of fact, not all humans *are* capable of holy love. Some might enter this world with such severe disabilities that they seem unable to express it and even to receive it, and others seem to go so far down the path of sinful narcissism that they appear incapable of empathy. There is much more that needs to be said, but the basic point made here is about the nature that is common to human persons. It may well be that something blocks that capacity in various conditions. In the first case, this something might be beyond the control of the person; in the second case, it may be that the blockage was put into place by the person. This would not mean that the capacity itself is not intrinsic to human nature — but it would mean that special divine action is necessary to remove that barrier so that the human nature can function properly again. And here we dare not limit the grace of God, and we dare not limit our horizons in such ways that obscure eschatological realities and possibilities.*

Conclusion

In this paper I have argued that human nature includes the capacity for holy love. The doctrine of Creation itself — and the doctrine of the Triune God upon which it rests — is amazingly good news!

Thomas H. McCall is Tennent Professor of Theology at Asbury Theological Seminary. Previously he served as a pastor in Michigan and Alaska and taught at Trinity Evangelical Divinity School, Asbury University, and the University of St Andrews.

---

* Discussion of these matters would take us far afield, but there is good reason to think that those who suffer from such blockage and thus lack the capability through all of this life may be free from such barriers in the life to come.

CHAPTER FOUR

Holy Love: An Old Testament Perspective

Victor P. Hamilton

Tribute

It has been my privilege to know Bill Ury ever since he stepped onto the campus of Asbury College as a new student sometime in the mid-70s. One could quickly discern that Bill was the type of student who would easily warm the heart of any professor. He was bright, intelligent, and curious, attributes a college professor delighted to see manifested in their students. More importantly, Bill demonstrated a deep, mature faith in his Christ, well beyond that of many other entering freshmen at college, and a faith that only continued to grow over his undergraduate years. I believe it was during his time at Asbury, under the presidency of Dr. Dennis Kinlaw, that Bill began to take a deeper interest in and commitment to the Wesleyan emphasis on sanctification and the call of God on all of His people to live a holy, Christlike life.

Bill has continued that passion in his teaching, preaching, and writing over the decades since graduation. I have had the privilege of sharing the platform with him in camp meetings and Bible conferences, and have always been challenged, stretched, and often convicted, by the depth of biblical and theological content and coherence (and urgency!) in those messages. To put it in a nutshell, Bill Ury is what we once called a "holiness preacher." To be sure, the emphasis on holy love is ubiquitous in Bill's sermons. More importantly, in my judgment, than sermonic, classroom brilliance is the demonstration of holy love that I have observed in Bill's life, in his marriage to his beloved Diane, and in their children. "Well done, thou good and faithful servant," I say.

Essay

"Whenever Israel would make a festival [at the Jerusalem temple]
they [the priests] would roll back the curtain for them
and show them the Cherubim who were embracing each other,
and say to them, 'Look! God's love for you
is as the love of a man and woman.'" *

When one uses the expression "the love of God," that phrase has a twofold meaning. First, one may take the phrase as a subjective

---

* Babylonian Talmud, *Yoma* 54a.

genitive. That is, the love of God is the love received from God, the love God gives. Or one may take the phrase to be an objective genitive. That is, the love of God is the love directed to and given to God, the love God receives. The first part of this essay will focus on the love God gives; then I will shift to an emphasis on the love God receives.

If most parishioners were asked which is more prominent in the Old Testament, the wrath of God or the love of God, the overwhelming majority would vote for the former. To a certain degree that is understandable. One scholar has found 714 references in the Old Testament to anger, 518 of which refer to God's anger.[*] References to love, divine and human, are not nearly so prolific.

It is interesting to note that in some recent Old Testament theologies the discussion of divine love is rather limited. I cite three examples. The first is Walter Brueggemann's work.[†] In a 750-page text there are four pages on the subject (pages 414-417). The second is John Goldingay's massive three volumes on Old Testament theology.[‡] In these volumes there are only brief discussions of "Loving Yahweh" and "Delighting in Yahweh." The longest treatment (2:108-134) touches explicitly on love only tangentially. My third example is Dennis Kinlaw's lectures.[§] I note in his index that there are 38 page references to "law," but no entries for "love." To be sure, none of these authors would deny the presence of holy love in the First Testament, and they certainly allude to it when

---

[*]   Bruce Baloian, *Anger in the Old Testament* (New York: Peter Lang, 1992) 89.

[†]   W. Brueggemann, *Theology of the Old Testament: Testimony, Dispute, Advocacy* (Minneapolis: Fortress Press, 1997).

[‡]   J. Goldingay, *Old Testament Theology* (Downer's Grove, IL: InterVarsity Press, 3 vols., 2003, 2006, 2009).

[§]   Dennis F Kinlaw, *Yahweh is God Alone: Lectures in Old Testament Theology.* ed. John Oswalt (Wilmore, KY: Francis Asbury Society. 2010).

discussing subjects like election or covenant, or Hebrew words like *hesed.*

Where do we go to start our search for holy love in Scripture? The best place to start is the Book of Deuteronomy. It is the "love book" of the Pentateuch/Torah if not of the whole Old Testament.* There are scattered uses of love language in Genesis-Numbers. Most of them are about parental love or spousal love, but none about God loving anybody or being loved by anybody. We do read, for example, that Abraham "feared" God (Genesis 22:12), but never that he "loved" God. There are two references in later Scripture (Isaiah 41:8; 2 Chronicles 20:7 and see James 2:23) to Abraham as "friend/lover of God." Interestingly, the Septuagint read the Hebrew consonantal text *'hb* not as an active participle as in the Masoretic Text with Abraham as subject and God as object, but as a passive participle with God as subject and Abraham as object.†

In contrast to these first four books of the Pentateuch, the fingerprints of divine love are all over Deuteronomy. My New International Version translation (1978 edition) lists 32 uses of "love/loved/loves" in Deuteronomy, and the vast majority of those are about either God's love for His chosen Israel, or Israel's love for their God. I suggest there is a parallel to this in the New Testament. The only person in the Synoptic gospels that Jesus is said to love is the so-called rich, young ruler, and only in the Markan version at that (see Mark 10:21). Contrastingly, divine love language is all over the Gospel of John. We can say that when it comes to explicit, divine love language, what John is to the Synoptic gospels in the

---

* See Jacqueline Lapsley, "Feeling Our Way: Love for God in Deuteronomy," *Catholic Biblical Quarterly* 65 (2003) 350-369.

† M Goshen-Gottstein, "Abraham — Lover or Beloved of God," in *Love and Death in the Ancient Near East,"* eds. J.H. Marks and R. M. Good (Guilford, CT: Four Quarters, 1987) 101-104.

New Testament, Deuteronomy is to Genesis — Numbers in the Old Testament.

Why, all of a sudden is there an explosion of divine love language in Deuteronomy? I am not sure there is an absolute answer to that. A number of scholars have appealed to love language in other literature from the larger biblical world. In particular, they draw attention to what are known as the Tel el-Amarna letters. These letters/correspondences dating to the fourteenth century BC from the leaders of Canaanite city states to the superior Pharaoh in Egypt requesting help to fight off those who are trying to topple them. I cite a portion from three of these texts translated in the Moran article. A local leader, facing an insurrection from malcontents, writes to the Pharaoh, "Half of [the city] *loves* the son of 'Abdi-Ashirta [the rebel ringleader], and half of it [*loves*] my lord."* A later use of this same sort of terminology comes from the seventh century BC. Esarhaddon, king of Assyria, uncertain whether after his death his people will be as loyal to his son and successor as they were to him, writes to his subjects, "You will *love* as yourselves Ashurbanipal." In a similar text Ashurbanipal, now king but facing the possibility of a fraternal revolt, compels his subjects under oath to make this promise: "The king of Assyria, our lord, we will *love*."

The one place in the Old Testament where "love" is used in a similar way to describe a relationship between two "heads of state" is 1 Kings 5:1-12, the covenant between Solomon and the neighboring Hiram, king of Tyre, a reciprocal relationship between the two nations started by David. Verse 1 (Hebrew verse 15) states that Hiram had always been "on friendly terms with David" (NIV).

---

* The seminal article on the possible connection between the Amarna Tablets and Scripture is William L. Moran, "The Ancient Near Eastern Background of the Love of God in Deuteronomy," *Catholic Biblical Quarterly* 25 (1963) 77-87.

The expression, "on friendly terms," is actually the participial form of the familiar Hebrew verb "love" ('*oheb*). It is the exact same verb and verbal form that we saw in the above two passages (Isaiah 41:8 and 2 Chronicles 20:7) that speak of Abraham as "God's friend/ lover." Obviously, the Kings passage does not imply, as do the Isaiah and Chronicles verses, any sort of deep affection between these two monarchs. It simply means both parties were benefitting from this give-and-take agreement.

What is glaringly missing from any of the above cuneiform texts is any suggestion that love between two parties, one more powerful, one less powerful, is a two-way street. All the love comes from servant to master. And it is love not in the sense of feelings of affection. Rather, it is loyalty born by fear of consequences if you are not loyal.

In bold contrast, one sees very quickly that the Old Testament repeatedly affirms Yahweh's love for Israel. For example, I count 27 references to God's "unfailing love" (often the NIV's rendering of the Hebrew word *hesed)* just in the book of Psalms. However, I wish to land on one reference in Deuteronomy that underscores God's holy love magnificently. It is Deuteronomy 7:7-8: "The LORD did not *set his affection on* you and chose you because you were more numerous than other peoples...But it was because the LORD *loved* you and kept the oath he swore to your forefathers..." (italics added). The Hebrew verb behind, "set one's affection on," is *hashaq*. It carries the idea of "have a deep desire for something/somebody," or "to take delight in something/ somebody." In four instances the verb is used in an erotic/marital sense to speak of an intense desire of a man for a woman. (1) See Genesis 34:8, Shechem longing for Dinah; (2) Deuteronomy 21:11, the male Israelite who is "attracted to" (NIV) a woman who has been captured; (3) Deuteronomy 25:7, the brother who has no passionate feelings for (NIV lamely, "does not want to") the widow of his late brother; (4)

Esther 2:14, potential wives were not invited back to the Persian king's chambers unless he was deeply attracted to (NIV, "pleased with") them.

Is it not fascinating that Deuteronomy would employ a verb with such nuances as a deep, passionate feelings for and attraction to a lover to describe Yahweh's relationship to Israel "an affair of the heart"? I cannot find a verse in the Old Testament that says essentially the same thing as John 3:16, God's love for the whole world. What we do find is God's amorous, love affair with his chosen Israel. We have all heard about and read about the four Greek words for love: *storge, philia,* e*ros,* and *agape.* It is a given that Christian tradition will privilege the last of these four as divine, agape love, that highlights God's undifferentiated love for the whosoever. However, in some Jewish writings, but by no means in all or even in most, there is a tendency to privilege God's erotic love, that is, His all-consuming, all-out, passionate love for His chosen.[*]

The biblical focus on the all-consuming love of God for Israel, seen in the Psalter and Deuteronomy, continues with some of the prophets. Three of them (Hosea, Jeremiah, and Ezekiel) will describe Yahweh's covenant with Israel as a marriage. The first two chapters of Hosea are rich with this imagery. The Lord instructs the prophet to marry an unfaithful wife who bears three sons, all of whom are given names that bespeak the rupture between faithful Yahweh and unfaithful Israel. Will that rupture lead to divorce? It seems as if the Lord comes perilously close to that option when He says, "I

---

[*] A prime example of a text that draws a sharp distinction between Jewish *eros* and Christian *agape* is Michael Wyschogrod, *Body of Faith* (North Vale, NJ: Jason Aaronson, 1983). This is not the place to debate this distinction, but for starters I recommend Leora Batnitzky's essay "Election and Affection: On God's Sovereignty and Human Action" in *The Call of Abraham: Essays on the Election of Israel in Honor of Jon D. Levenson,* eds. Gary A. Anderson and Joel S. Kaminsky (Notre Dame, IN: University of Notre Dame Press, 2013) 309-329.

will no longer show love to the house of Israel" (Hosea1:6b), or "she is not my wife* and I am not her husband" (Hosea 2:2a). Yes, the spouse guilty of betrayal must pay some sort of price for that betrayal (see Hosea 2:9-13). In the long run, however, God's mercy and incredible love trump justice and punitive action. The romance is rekindled thanks to the benevolent generosity of Yahweh (Hosea 2:14-23).†

Jeremiah, the only individual in the Old Testament divinely called to lifelong bachelorhood (Jeremiah 16:2), also uses the marriage concept as a way of thinking about Yahweh's loving, covenantal relationship with chosen Israel. Unlike in Hosea, in Jeremiah the metaphorical wife of the Lord is at the start of the marriage faithful and loving (Jer. 2:2-3). But after a while, things go downhill. It seems here that divorce, unlike in Hosea, actually happens. In Jeremiah 3:7, 14 and 4:1 the brokenhearted Yahweh implores His remarried ex-bride to return to Him, her first lover. But there's a problem. According to Deuteronomy 24:1-4. a husband is not allowed to remarry his wife if after the divorce she has remarried a second husband. Is the Almighty caught on the horns of a dilemma? Can God break His own law? Fretheim in his Jeremiah commentary says movingly, "God cannot simply say, 'I must obey the law,' and walk away from the people of Israel. Israel can bring nothing to the table to force the hand of God. But, wonder of wonders, God allows Israel a place at the table!"‡

---

* References to Israel to as "God's wife" will inevitably lead people to think of Israel as a "she." However, Israel in the Bible is always, grammatically. masculine.

† Interestingly, the one thing in Scripture God is said to be "slow" at is getting angry. See the phrase "slow to anger" in Exodus 34:6, and in numerous other passages that also use this phrase. If God has any kind of an anger problem, it is that He gets angry so slowly, so incrementally. James 1:19 suggests that this is a good way in which His adherents can imitate Him. The one thing the Bible says God is not slow at is keeping His promises. See 2 Peter 3:9.

‡ Terence E. Fretheim, *Jeremiah*. Smyth & Helwys Bible Commentary (Macon, GA:

Ezekiel 16 has been described as the closest chapter in the Old Testament of an equivalent to John 3:16 when it comes to a picture of God's unmerited and lavish love. Israel appears in her early days after birth as the bloody and forsaken infant of two Canaanite parents. Yet, God is attracted to her, eventually falls in love with her, and then marries her (Ezek. 16:8). Indeed, Yahweh was a giving spouse to His bride (Ezek. 16:9-14). Alas, Israel, in spite of all these benefactions, played the harlot (Ezekiel 16:15). Infidelity always comes with a price (Ezekiel 16:35-43). But as in Hosea and Jeremiah divine anger is not the last word. The last word in Ezekiel 16 is divine forgiveness, restoration, and renewal. Such is God's holy and compassionate love.

As a final citation from Old Testament Scripture, I cite the intriguing Song of Solomon. Rabbi Akiva (Akiba), a rabbinic sage from the end of the first and into the second centuries AD, when reflecting on this book said, "If all the writings are holy, the Song of Songs is holy of holies."[*] Commentators have gone back and forth on whether this is an allegory on God's love for Israel (or Christ's love for His body, the church), or is simply a powerful, sensual and erotic narrative involving two human lovers, either married or on their way to marriage. If one allows this book to stand by itself without any connections to the rest of Scripture, then I think the argument favors the latter approach. But if one attempts to see this book as part and parcel of, and in agreement with, the rest of Scripture's teachings on covenantal love, then just possibly one can interpret this Song as a narrative about God's love affair with Israel. Jon Levenson pointedly asks,

---

Smyth & Helwys, 2002) 75.
[*]   Robert Alter, *Strong As Death Is Love* (New York: W. W. Norton & Company, 2015) 3.

Who…could these two passionate lovers possibly be? Let us put the question in terms of the rest of the Hebrew Bible: Where…do we find an intense love in which the lovers are separated much of the time, the male of the two is not continually accessible, the identities of the lovers seem to shift in various situations, powerful external forces oppose and threaten the romance, and the consummation of that relationship seems to be maddeningly postponed? Put that way, the question nearly answers itself: the only such romance is that of God and Israel.[*]

It should not come as a surprise that Deuteronomy is replete with admonitions to love the Lord. After all, the bulk of Deuteronomy is three sermons or exhortations Moses delivers east of the Jordan to his people as they prepare to enter Canaan. And it's not just love the Lord a little, but love Him with everything with which you can show your love for Him. For references to "love the Lord your God with "all your…" see 6:5; 10:12; 11:13; 13:3; 30:6.

Possibly the best known verses in Deuteronomy are 6:4-5, often called the *Shema* which is the Hebrew word for "Hear" in "Hear, O Israel: The LORD our God is one. Love the LORD your God with all your heart and with all your soul and with all your strength."[†]

* Jon Levenson, *The Love of God: Divine Gift, Human Gratitude, and Mutual Faithfulness in Judaism* (Princeton, NJ: Princeton University Press, 2016) 131-132. I have found all the writings of Professor Levenson very stimulating and creative and recommend them to readers of this essay.

† It is possible to translate these two verses in different ways. The most recent and suggestive studies I have seen of the *Shema* are those of Walter Moberly. See (1) "'YHWH is One': The Translation of the Shema," in *Studies in the Pentateuch*, ed J. A. Emerton, Supplements to *Vetus Testamentum* 41 (Leiden: Brill, 1990) 209-215, reprinted in R. W. L. Moberly, *From Eden to Golgatha: Essays in Biblical Theology*, South Florida Studies in the History of Judaism 52 (Atlanta: Scholars Press, 1992), 75-81; (2) "Toward an Interpretation of the Shema," in *Theological Exegesis: Essays in Honor of Brevard S. Childs*, eds. Christopher R. Seitz and Kathryn Greene-McCreight (Grand Rapids, MI, 1999),124-144; (3) The chapter "A Love Supreme"

Along with these two verses there are a good number elsewhere in Deuteronomy that link love for God with obedience to His laws and commandments, for example, 10:12-13; 11:1; 19:9; 30:16. That is one way of demonstrating one's love for their Lord. That is no different from Jesus' "If you love me, you will obey what I command" (John 14:15). But can there be obedience without love? Ask any child. Ask anybody in the military. If obeying the laws and commandments of Scripture scrupulously is the acid test, the primary test, of a holy life and love for God, then as Steve DeNeff has said, "The Pharisees would be our friends and not our enemies. The rich young ruler would be in heaven and the dying thief in hell."*

I believe a good argument can be made for the fact that love of God relates not only to behavior but also to affection.† Who would want a religion whose God is primarily interested in the strict obedience of His vassals? As the call to holiness, so is the call to love God. Both calls are more about invitation than they are about intimidation ("you better be holy/loving or else…").

There is one difference in how holiness language appears in Leviticus and in Deuteronomy. In the former the phrase that occurs is "You [plural] shall be holy because I, the LORD your God, am holy" (Lev. 11: 44-45; 19:2; 20:7, 26; 26:8).‡ In contrast

---

in *Old Testament Theology: Reading the Hebrew Bible as Christian Scripture* (Grand Rapids, MI: Baker Academic, 2013), 7-40. Moberly's own interpretive rendering of the Shema is, "Hear, O Israel: YHWH our God, YHWH is the one and only. So you should love YHWH your God with all your thinking, with all your longing, and with all your striving" (2013:24).

* Steve DeNeff, *More Than Forgiveness: A Contemporary Call to Holiness Based on the Life of Jesus Christ* (Indianapolis, IN: Wesleyan Publishing House, 2002) 103. A few pages later he states, "Obedience is love's final test, but never its first" (110).

† See Lapsley's article mentioned in footnote 6 and Levenson's book mentioned in footnote 14, especially pp. 21-29, "Action and Affection." Also, Bill T. Arnold, "The Love-Fear Antinomy in Deuteronomy 5 — 11," *Vetus Testamentum* 61 (2011) 551-569.

‡ We refer to the Hebrew Bible sometimes as the Masoretic TEXT (MT), That title refers

to this language, Deuteronomy consistently refers to God's chosen with, "You [singular] are a holy people/a people holy" (7:6; 14:2,21; 26:19; 28:9, a phrase unique to Deuteronomy in the Old Testament).* Hence, Leviticus' "You shall be holy" becomes in Deuteronomy "You are holy." In the first holiness is a goal. In the second holiness is a present reality. Here is the motive for obedience. Not love out of morbid fear lest the Overlord withdraw His welcomed and necessary benefactions. Rather, a holy person or a holy people will spontaneously and simultaneously love their Lord lavishly and serve their Lord loyally.

The picture I have tried to paint from the Old Testament is: Holy love from a holy God for a holy people, and in response holy love from a holy people for a holy God.

Victor Hamilton was professor of Old Testament studies for 36 years, from 1971 to 2007, at Asbury College/University in Wilmore, KY. He started teaching at Asbury a few months after receiving his doctorate in Mediterranean Studies from Brandeis University in Waltham, MA. One of his greatest memories from his days of teaching undergraduates was preaching in the chapel services

---

to a group of Jewish scholars known as the Masoretes who, between 500-900AD, provided vowel points (along with a few other items) for the consonantal Hebrew text to aid in pronunciation. Not wanting to add anything to the sacred text, they instead added "point" vowels, that is, dots and dashes above and below the consonant. How they vocalized these "holy" verses from Leviticus is most interesting. When the adjective "holy" refers to human holiness, they vocalized the "o" in the Hebrew adjective *qadosh* with what grammarians call a "defective" spelling. But when the adjective "holy" refers to God's holiness, they vocalized the "o" in *qadosh* with what grammarians call a 'full" or "plene" spelling. In transliteration, the "o" in "holy, *qadosh*" for our holiness would have a line over the top of the vowel, while the sign over the vowel for divine holiness would have a circumflex. This was their way of saying that holiness leads to godlikeness, but it does not lead to God. Holiness confers character, but it does not confer divinity.

* This time the Masoretes pointed the "o" vowel in *qadosh* as a "full/plene" vocalization even though the reference was to human holiness. The reason is simple: In Deuteronomy, unlike in Leviticus, human holiness does not appear in proximity to divine holiness.

at least once a year, and often more than once a year, for 40 years, from 1972 to 2012. In addition to classroom teaching, he has written a number of Old Testament commentaries. These include two Handbooks, one on the Pentateuch, and the other on the Historical Books. Vic has also written a two-volume commentary on Genesis for the NICOT series, and a commentary on Exodus which he wrote in his early years after retirement from Asbury. Vic has been married to his "dear Shirley" since 1965.

CHAPTER FIVE

Holy Love and the Church

G. Stephen Blakemore

Tribute

Aristotle once said, "Wishing to be friends is quick work, but friendship is a slow ripening fruit." That evaluation comes to mind when I think of my long-standing relationship with Bill. We met one another at Asbury College and formed our first bonds of acquaintance and friendship competing as teammates on Asbury's track and field team. We ran on relay teams together and I always was handing the baton to him for three years. Across the years we were in college, Bill and I grew close, but it was in our years together in seminary that our friendship deepened. Reflecting on the challenges of following Jesus as twenty-somethings who were learning how to be men of faith, praying for one another, studying the Bible together, and discussing theological issues — these centered our friendship around living for the Triune God. Since those early years I can testify to the reality that his friendship in my life has been a "slow ripening fruit." In life's struggles, he has been a constant source of encouragement, direction, and insight. Through life's joys, he has been a friend who would rejoice with me when I rejoiced. When I joined the faculty of Wesley Biblical Seminary, he was a great "cheerleader" for a novice professor. My life is richer because he has been my friend for so long. It is a blessing to have a friend, but especially so when your friend is someone you admire as a man, and a man of God. I am thankful to God that Bill Ury is my friend.

Essay

The *People of God* — the One who is Holy Love — this concept is central to the narratives of the Old and New Testaments. Being God's people is a calling and a gift, first to Israel and then the disciples of Jesus. We cannot forget either the grace nor the vocation involved in being God's people, which began with God's calling upon Abraham, ran through, in a preparatory way, Israel's establishment as God's special treasure at Sinai, and was fulfilled in the life, death, resurrection, and ascension of Jesus of Nazareth. Having a particular people present in the sin-wrecked, fallen creation to be the locus of His presence and self-revelation is central to God's saving economy. Being His presence and messenger, the Church is central to redeeming grace. Understanding what it means to be the people of God in Christ, therefore, is not a secondary concern of theology, but touches the heart of God's grace and revelation.

For Christian theology it is hard to overstate the reality that the Incarnation of Christ, His sacrifice, resurrection, and ascension all entail the creation of the Church. Jesus's language recorded in St. John's Gospel reveals this. He describes Himself as the Vine which has fruit-bearing branches.* One can wonder about where the identity of the Vine terminates, and the identity of the branches begins in such a metaphor. Our life is *in Him,* so we are integral to the purpose of the Vine, and His Life in the Father is to our identity. Paul describes the redeeming *and* redemptive relation between Jesus and the Church in Romans — "the first born among many brethren."† Hence, the Resurrection is about more than Jesus' identity and vindication. He is to be a recreator and forerunner of many others who are to be *in Him* and *like Him* in His victory. The great apostle also declares the Church to be the "fullness of Him [Christ]."‡ In all, the gospel proclamation about Christ's incarnation, living, teaching, dying, being raised, ascension, sending with the Father the Holy Spirit finds its *telos* in His final return to bring to Creation a restoration that involves the Bride of the Lamb descending as a blessing on Creation. The Church's soteriological centrality deserves full consideration, because it is identified with Jesus, and in Jesus with the Triune God.

---

* The Gospel of John chapter 15.

† Romans 8:29. It is instructive to note that in this passage the predestination of those God "foreknew" is not merely to be justified, but to be sanctified and even perhaps "divinized" to the image of His God's Son. This is the essence of salvation, not forgiveness of sins and the forbearance of judgment. This does not settle the debates between Calvinists and Arminians in Evangelicalism, but it does reorient the discussion of what salvation actually *is* — to become a partaker of Christ's nature by grace.

‡ Ephesians 1:23.

Where Are We Today

Ecclesiology became a concern in the Western world about seventy-five years ago as a twentieth century ecumenical movement.* No doubt driven by the horrors of two world wars when people from nations shaped by Christian faith slaughtered one another, The World Council of Churches was formed to press the question of what spiritual relationship and vocational responsibilities Christians and Christian communions have together when also citizens of different, competing nations. They wondered why the Church's life and the common confession of faith in the Holy One of Holy Love was ineffectual against such barbarity. Following this mid-century movement, the last half of the twentieth century saw a further and deeper renewal of engagement between traditions regarding the relation of various Christian communions in the faith.† The transitional years into the twentieth-first century produced dialogues rooted in a common Christian desire to recover theological orthodoxy as new intra-Christian discourse took place.‡

Despite these things, the observations of Father Georges Florovsky at the first gathering of the World Council of Churches are still relevant today. He described ecclesiology as still in a pre-

---

* Veli-Matti Kärkkäinen, *Introduction to Ecclesiology*, (Downers Grove, IL: IVP) 7-8. "No other movement in the history of the Christian church, perhaps with the exception of the Reformation, has shaped the thinking and practice of Christendom as much as the modern movement for Christian unity."

† In addition to the modern ecumenical movement, one could not overestimate the effect of Vatican II and its rather generous attitude toward non-Roman communions. As well, one could note the enormous contribution made by the figure of John Paul the Great, in his outreach to Orthodox and Protestants. However, one would be historically naïve to ignore the powerful effect that the ministry of the Reverend Billy Graham had in America, at least, with his evangelical preaching and revival campaigns that tended to bring believers together from across the spectrum of traditions, even Roman Catholics. A quick search of internet sources will reveal the extent of Graham's appeal even to Catholics.

‡ See, James S. Cutsinger, Ed, *Reclaiming the Great Tradition* (Downers Grove, IL: IVP, 1997).

theological stage of development, noting that while everyone speaks of the Church, no thorough *conciliar* statements exist about its nature or boundaries.[*] While Christians can agree that we are all *Christians* in some sense, we cannot agree in exactly what way we are united by common faith as one "Church."

Ecclesiology has, however, received serious treatment in the individual work of some of the West's most consequential theologians. Wolfhart Pannenberg from the Lutheran tradition and Jurgen Moltmann of the Reformed heritage have offered insightful and ecumenically sensitive ecclesiological reflections as Protestants.[†] Miroslav Wolf has written from a perspective that takes the Reformed and the Pentecostal traditions *together* seriously.[‡] James McClendon has provided thoughts on the contributions that a self-consciously Baptist ecclesiology can offer.[§] Michael Ramsey's work from the early twentieth century on the Church from an ecumenically-sensitive Anglican perspective has been reprinted.[¶] Additionally, one can read John Zizioulas from the Orthodox or Avery Dulles from the Roman Catholic traditions.[**] Even Pope Benedict XVI felt the need to clarify Catholic teaching on the relationship between believers, saying that believers from other traditions outside of Roman Catholicism do not lack the grace of salvation, but only constitute ecclesial communities,

---

[*]   Colin W. Williams, "The Church, New Directions," *Theology Today*, no 4, (1969): 11.

[†]   Wolfhart Pannenberg and Geoffrey Bromiley, Tr, Systematic *Theology*, Vol 3 (Grand Rapids, MI: Eerdmans, 2009. And Jurgen Moltmann, *The Church in the Power of the Spirit* (Minneapolis, MN: Fortress Press, 1993).

[‡]   Miroslav Wolf, *After our Likeness: The Church as the Image of the Trinity* (Grand Rapids, MI: Eerdmans, 1997).

[§]   James Wm. McClendon, Jr, *Witness: Systematic Theology* Vol 3 (Nashville, TN: Abingdon Press, 2000).

[¶]   Michael Ramsey, *Gospel and the Catholic Church* (Eugene, OR: Wipf and Stock. 2009).

[**]   Zizioulas, *Being as Communion: Studies in Personhood and the Church* (Yonkers, NY: St. Vladimir's Press, 1997) "The Ecclesiological Presuppositions of the Holy Eucharist," *Nicolaus* 10 (1982) 333-49. Avery Dulles, *Models of the Church*, (Garden City, NY: Image Books, 2002).

as they lack the full range of God's gifts only present in the Roman Catholic Church.* Recently, Howard Snyder, William Abraham, and Jason Vickers, from the Methodist tradition, have dropped new considerations into the discussion of the nature of the Church.†

The Tragedy of the Practical

These theological treatments are quite important, but the insights they offer have not shaped very significantly the perspectives and practices of the foot-soldiers — pastors and leaders within the laity, since the most works for local church leaders focus on practical issues of leadership and ministry.‡ Of course, proper operational structures and missional practices of the Church are important, yet to launch prematurely into discussion of fruitful function in ministry while not attending to clarity about the nature and identity of the Church and how to know where and how Christ's people are instantiated is regrettable, perhaps detrimental. Surely what the Church *is* should inform our thinking about what the Church should *do* and why it should *do* those things and not others. Then the question of *how* emerges properly.

Millard Erickson observed decades ago two socio-cultural, theological dynamics that produced the primarily practical

---

* As unsatisfactory as we Protestants might find this, it is a welcome acknowledgement that saving grace extends beyond Roman Catholicism.

† Howard A Snyder, *Signs of the Spirit: How God Reshapes the Church* (Eugene, OR: Wipf and Stock, 1997). William J. Abraham and Jason E. Vickers, eds. *Canonical Theism* (Grand Rapids, MI: Eerdmans, 2008).

‡ The phenomenal success at the end of the 20th century of Rick Warren's work, *The Purpose Driven Church: Every Church Is Big In God's Eyes* (Grand Rapids, MI: Zondervan, 1995), written for pastors and lay leaders in local churches is an example of this practical orientation. While phenomenally helpful and a means of grace, this book put the issue in terms of *purpose* and suggest practical strategies is to move from consideration of essence and identity to a treatment of function. Other practical works on the Church from the last century and the first part of the twenty-first century would be those of Leonard Sweet and Brian McLauren.

orientation that is present in most ecclesiological thinking. The first is the theological reorientation that emerged accentuating the doctrine of God's immanence to the attenuation of the doctrines of transcendence and aseity. This shift in focus, he argued, caused the attention of persons writing on the nature of the Church to be captured by questions "about the Church in terms of its relationship to other entities, for example, secular society." This shift of emphasis on what God is doing in the world at large (immanent providence) rather than God's essence (transcendent aseity), meant that "more attention has been given to the mission of the church than to its identity and limits or boundaries." The second dynamic noted was the radical allergy to metaphysics by twentieth century philosophers whose thought life was adapted to the atmosphere of Positivism and Empiricism. As modern theology took clues from non-trinitarian philosophy (rather than revelation), theologians were "less interested in the essence of the Church, what it 'really is' or 'ought to be,' than in its embodiment, what it concretely is or dynamically is becoming."*

No focus upon the mission of the Church is to be denigrated, for Jesus Himself declared to His followers, "as the Father has sent me, so I send you." Yet, failure to deal with the Church's *nature* and focus on the Church's *mission* can lead to a kind of cultural "Babylonian captivity." Focus upon the "how" questions without

---

* Millard Erickson, *Christian Theology, 1ᵗ ed.* (Ada, MI: Baker Academic), 1027 — 1028. No doubt, the hegemonic influence of mainline Protestantism in the 20th century also created a context in which the existence of the Church was simply taken for granted and its importance assumed (even if unexamined). Also, given American Protestantism's penchant for individualism, the notion of examining the metaphysical nature of the Church was perhaps invisible to theologians' eyes, given that the starting point of individualism arrives at and evaluation of the church in voluntarist terms. Concerning Erickson's last observation, consider the language much celebrated in current literature on "the emerging Church" or "progressive Christianity.

serious consideration of the identity of the Church can lead to preoccupation with what the situation of the world is "demanding" of the Church, resulting, as Pannenberg noted, in our defining Christian witness in relation to the culture in which the Church exists.* Today, it is so-called Progressive Christianity which insists that Critical Race Theory and the social justice movements are definitively calling the Church to repent, because of "what God is doing." What about tomorrow? Reinterpreting the gospel and the calling of the Church by cultural developments risks producing a "baptized echo" of secular values. However, the gospel is a totalizing worldview, and only in rediscovering theologically that we are the People of God with a specific theological view of reality can we truly serve the world.†

Hope in the "Old" for New Understanding

Recalling the Ante-Nicene Fathers' work could help reorient us, since they never addressed the Church's nature or ministry in isolation from reflections on the Trinity and soteriology. In the

---

* Wolfhart Pannenberg, "When Everything Is Permitted," *First Things* 80 (February, 1980) 26 — 30. "Protestantism has understood itself to be working in tandem with the development of the modern world. This is notably true of liberal Protestantism, what is often called the "cultural Protestantism" once dominant in much of Europe and North America. This Protestantism is reluctant to differ from the prevailing values of the general culture. Indeed, it feels it has a proprietorial interest in those values. This attitude can be traced to the Reformation, and especially to Luther's doctrine that the Christian is fulfilling his divine vocation by doing the work he is called to in the secular sphere. This was "in sharpest contrast to the Roman Catholic view that there are, for instance in monasticism, special vocations to holiness. Moreover, and very important to our discussion of moral authority, Protestantism took credit for the development of modern ideas of liberty and human rights. As a result, Protestants viewed adaptation to modern culture not as a course of moral compromise but as a course of fidelity to their heritage."

† As Stanley Hauerwas famously reminded us, the Church exists to tell us what our real needs are, not to respond to our felt needs.

second and third centuries reference to the Church is (exclusively) considered an extension of the doctrine of the Holy Spirit. The *Apostolic Constitutions* from Hippolytus is exemplary in the third baptismal question: "Do you believe in the Holy Spirit *in the Church?*" Irenaeus's theology of the identity and nature of the Church is emblematic, as well: "For where the Church is, there is also the Spirit of God. And where the Spirit of God is, there is also the Church and all grace; for the Spirit is the Truth." Cyril of Jerusalem in the fourth century described the church as "one, holy, catholic and apostolic" (*Catechetical Lectures*), thus expanding but not negating the focus on the Holy Spirit. Not until Peter Lombard's influential work, *Sentences,* can one find a definitive shift, but only from Pneumatology to Christology. Discussion about the Church was still theo-centric and trinitarian.

Even Nicaea itself was addressing more than a crucial theological controversy. The debated doctrine was intimately entangled with a concern to define the Church's true boundaries by trinitarian confessions. The Council's precipitating conflict was between various churches, not academic theologians. Disputes had arisen over the identity of the *Logos* in relationship to God the Father. A regional council called by Alexander, Bishop of Alexandria was convened to resolve a debate between the bishop and a presbyter, Arius, that arose after Alexander preached a sermon to explicate the *similarity* of the Son to the Father. Arius heard in this a revival of Sabellianism. Appalled by perceived modalism in Alexander's teaching, he rebutted the bishop, arguing "if the Father begat the Son, He that was begotten had a beginning of existence: and from this it is evident, that there was a time when the Son was not. It therefore necessarily follows, that He had His substance from nothing."[*] Ironically, the future anathematized heretic saw himself defending the Church's Apostolic faith, but the North African bishops demurred. Therefore, writing to Bishop Alexander of Constantinople, Alexandria's prelate charged Arius — rather vaguely — with heresy. Given Arius's popularity and influence in Antioch, the debate quickly became framed in terms of a struggle between the Antiochian churches and the Alexandria-centered congregations. Thus, a truly ecumenical council was required. Athanasius, Arius's counterpart, championed Alexandrian churches' insistence on the Son's divine equality with the Father. The conclusion: Nicaea produced a clear statement of the Faith that was discerned and declared to be truly orthodox and apostolic belief.[†]

This rehearsal is important to show that more was at stake in the minds of the participants than theological precision. Affirming continuity with historic confessions involved the questions of how to recognize the true Church and who the Church was to worship — identity and essence issues. Christian liturgies had since the days of the Apostles acknowledged Jesus to be worthy of worship as God Incarnate.[‡] Arius's Christology undercut the Church's sense of worship and, therefore, its identity, because the Church's existence and practice were inextricably tied to the question of the nature of God in Christ. Historically, if the Church's apostolic identity as the People of God was to be secured, orthodox bishops could not separate the Church's life from the correct affirmation and

---

[*] "Socrates of Constantinople," *Church History*, Bk1/5. www.newadvent.org/fathers/26011. htm.

[†] Regarding the Council's declaration of the "co-eternality" of the *Logos* and the Father, all but two bishops — Theonas of Marmarica and Secundus of Ptolemais — signed the creedal affirmations. They were stripped of ordination and excommunicated, along with Arius.

[‡] See Larry Hurtado, *The Origins of Christian Worship* (Grand Rapids: Eerdmans, 2000) for a good discussion of the binitarian shape that earliest Christian worship took.

worship of God as Trinity. Even subsequent conciliar decisions on the Scriptural canon itself revolved around which of the writings had been long utilized in the liturgies of the churches catholic, all of which were trinitarian in structure. The Church's confession and worship of the Trinity became the universally applicable discernment standard for being in the Church.[*]

Discussions about the identity and constitutive foundations of the Church do not emerge in isolation from trinitarian considerations until the years leading up to the Reformation, no doubt as a result of growing tensions that developed as renewal movements grew in medieval Europe that challenged the mediatorial hegemony of the Roman Catholic medieval hierarchy. "The first separate ecclesiological statements were *Tractatus de Ecclesia* of Johann of Ragusa and *Summa de Ecclesia* of John Torquemada, of the same period."[†] Not surprisingly, with the Reformation ecclesiology became prominent.[‡] The 1535 version of the *Loci* of Melanchthon added an individual section on the Church: "the Church is the congregation of saints, in which the gospel is rightly taught, and the sacraments are rightly administered."[§] This well-known Protestant

---

[*] However, the "victory" of Nicea was not decisive as the controversies continued over the next several centuries and Arian Christianity spread in the Germanic tribes especially.

[†] Karkkainen, 11. Surely it is a telling matter that Roman Catholic theologians felt compelled to write a separate ecclesiologies during the period that Catholic lay movements such as the *Devotio Moderna* began to create a spiritual renewal that was ultimately a threat to the idea of mediated faith in God. As well, there were the movements of John Hus and John Wycliffe threatening much of the Church's perceived authority.

[‡] So closely was one's salvation linked to being in the Church (Roman) that the Reformers had to establish a conception of the Church's identity that would give comfort to many who defected at the time of the Reformation, assuring them they were not *leaving* the One True Church. We do well to recall that at least with regard to Luther the original movement was a *reform* movement not a replacement endeavor.

[§] Pannenberg's observations are on point: "It has been said that here for the first time, on the basis of the new reformation beginning, Melanthon tried to project and develop a theology of the church as a whole." Pannenberg, *Systematic Theology*, vol 3 22. Also, see *Canonical Theism*, Abraham.

dictum defines the Church, not self-consciously in relationship to the Holy Trinity, but by reference to the persons comprising the Church (saints) and the practices (preaching and sacraments) of the Church. While not lacking theological content, such a description is primarily phenomenological and functional, which has marked Protestantism since.

An Ecclesiology of Holy Love

So, what *is* the Church as the People of God — the Holy Trinity of Holy Love? Knowing that will redirect our thoughts about everything else. As was shown above, the Fathers' reflections on the Church were deeply theological and soteriological rather than organizational or practical.* The writings of the contemporary theologians listed earlier have set out to return to this focus. Ecclesiology that starts with Jesus — the Incarnate Son as the revealer that God is the Trinity of Holy Love — and the apostolic witness should lead to the conclusion that the Church is to be far more than a mere *proclaiming* presence *to* the world, even more than a *discipling* presence *in* the world. The Church is a *participating* presence *for* the world. The New Testament's language of the Church as the body of Christ, the fullness of Christ, a dwelling place being built together in which God dwells by His Spirit, and partakers of the divine nature is not merely poetic.† A radical identification of God's People with the presence of God in Christ in the world is at work. It is not too much to say that the Church is the way the Holy

---

* The same thing could be applied to the insistence upon apostolic succession of bishops as inheritors of the teaching authority of the Apostles and protectors the Faith of the Church in the early centuries.

† I Corinthians 12:27, Ephesians 1:23 & 2:22, and II Peter 1:4.

One of Holy Love is "visibly" present. The Holy Spirit in believers' hearts is not just a power given by God but is the personal presence of the Trinity's Third Person in and among His People. Union with Christ, who is the Image of the invisible God and through whom we receive the Spirit, unites us with God and enlivens the Church as a "continuation" of the Incarnation. Furthermore, when one considers the description of the eschatological culmination in the Book of the Revelation, a mysterious and inescapable realization is suggested: the Church — the Bride of the Lamb — is central to the re-creation and salvation that the Triune God will bring to His broken creation.* The eschatological completion of the salvation inaugurated in the Incarnate life of the Son is identified with the Church's relationship with God in Christ. What is true *now* for God's children *will be* for all Creation.

Furthermore, a robust trinitarian doctrine of Creation (God as eternally, unbounded Holy Love) allows us to see the universe was created because the Trinity is utterly self-fulfilling in the fullness of the Three Persons sharing Divine Life. Needing nothing, Holy Love creates something not Himself for the purpose of giving Himself to it and for it. As creatures bearing the Image Holy Love, humanity's first experience of grace is not Christ's Incarnation but being made to be the image of God and able to receive and express Holy Love's love. Such a divine gift cannot be obliterated, but by the Fall we are alienated from our true human nature. Salvation, then, is rebirth that reorders our lives rightly, not just *before* God but *in* God's life. Alive in the Holy One, we are brought into relationship not just with God but with others in Christ. Christ as the perfect *image of the invisible God* came to baptize us in the Holy Spirit and restore to His Church the

---

* Revelation 21:2 — 10.

capacity to be *together* the image of the Trinity as the redeemed People of God, because God's triune essence is a mutual sharing in Love.

Space allows only a brief sketch of what seeing God as Holy Love requires for an adequate ecclesial self-consciousness. First, the Church's primary calling is to love the One who is holy love, *because He is holy love.* Communal adoration of the Triune God, in order to participate in divine life, must be the primary focus and priority of every congregation's worship, not primarily encouragement and discipleship of believers or sensitivity to seekers. In adoring worship, we declare a truth the world cannot know without our worship — life must be God-centered and God-receiving. Worship is witness!

Second, developing small groups that share life together and embody holy love in human relationships is essential for spiritual formation and discipleship in trinitarian faith. Such groups will prioritize studying theology and its implications, because practical, devotional matters cannot substitute for knowing God and God's nature. In such groups, confessing sins to one another as witness to the seriousness of sin against holy love would become natural; forgiveness of the penitent would express holy love's grace.

Third, evangelism and compassionate ministries will be seen as two-sides of one calling — offering the love of Holy Love to the world. Calling people to repent is an act of love as much as meeting needs. The last is easier, but fallen culture confuses and corrupts us, and confronting people's lifestyles and worldviews regarding gender, race, sexuality, greed, rage, and meaning, is to offer holy love's healing, recreating gift.

Fourth, local churches would move beyond self-referential, territorial values and practice *holy love* in Christ by intentionally worshipping and ministering regularly with other congregations from different Christian traditions. Though seeming small, such acts testify to God's new humanity in Christ and the eschatological promise of reconciliation, unity, and hope.

Finally, holy love will enable us to face our failures, defeat our temptations, forgive our wounders, love our enemies, receive strangers, and offer hope. We will begin to resemble holy love, who makes new life possible, and thereby, demands it.

G. Stephen (Steve) Blakemore is the Professor of Christian Thought at Wesley Biblical Seminary. He is also a senior fellow with the John and Charles Wesley Center for Christian Thought and Apologetics. He is married to Carolyn and together they have four grown sons and three grandchildren.

CHAPTER SIX

Holy Love and Pastoral Ministry

Reverend Sean Scribner

Tribute

From the fall of 2013 to the spring of 2017, I had the immense privilege of serving as the Associate Pastor to Dr. Bill Ury at Elizabeth City Evangelical Methodist Church in Elizabeth City, NC. Over the previous decade I had been deeply impacted by Dr. Ury from our time together at camp meetings, through long distance correspondence, and then as one of his students at Wesley Biblical Seminary in Jackson, MS. However, those three and a half years of serving together in the local church impacted me the most as I witnessed the self-giving heart of Jesus work in and through the yielded life of my pastor, teacher, mentor, and friend. That time of ministry left an indelible mark on my person that has molded and shaped me into the man and pastor that I am today.

In the summer of 2017, I was called into the lead pastor role upon Dr. Ury's departure, and on September 4, 2021 I had the honor of preaching a sermon at the church's 75th Anniversary Celebration. That sermon on Colossians 2:1-5 is what follows. The pastoral concern contained in this passage, that Christ's flock would come to know the fullness of the Good Shepherd, is the same concern I saw week in and week out in the life of Dr. Ury. He had agony for the same things as the apostle, as do all shepherds whose lives have been touched and filled by the holy love of God. That Christ is known fully through the truth of His Word and the fellowship of His Body was the constant refrain of Dr. Ury's life and ministry in Elizabeth City, and for that I will forever be grateful.

Essay
Knowing the Fullness of Christ*

"I want you to know how much I have agonized for you and for the church at Laodicea, and for many other believers who have never met me personally. I want them to be encouraged and knit together by strong ties of love. I want them to have complete confidence that they understand God's mysterious plan, which is Christ himself. In him lie hidden all the treasures of wisdom and knowledge. I am telling you this so no one will deceive you with well-crafted

---

* A sermon preached for the 75th Anniversary Celebration of Elizabeth City Evangelical Methodist Church in Elizabeth City, NC on September 4, 2021.

arguments. For though I am far away from you, my heart is with you. And I rejoice that you are living as you should and that your faith in Christ is strong" (Colossians 2:1-5 New Living Translation).

In our text, Paul wants the Christians at Colossae and the surrounding region to know how much he has agonized for them. The Greek word for agony is *agón*, and it evokes thoughts of an athletic contest that is both strenuous and demanding. Perhaps the word is best expressed here in this passage as a struggle of the soul, like the deep concern and effort a parent bears and exerts on behalf of their children. Paul was touched and moved on behalf of these Christians at the level of the heart, yet he had never even met them face to face. Why?

You might begin by pointing to Paul's connection to the Colossians through his fellow ministry partner and prisoner, Epaphras. He was one of the Colossians' own (Colossians 4:12) and had been the messenger who first presented the gospel to them (Colossians 1:6-7). This would make Paul something like the Colossians' spiritual grandfather who had invested interest in the churches that resulted from his disciple's ministry.

In addition to this personal connection, it is not hard to detect in the Pauline corpus his profound missionary and pastoral heart. He had received a special commission to be an apostle to the Gentiles, was called by Christ Himself to make the riches, glory, and mysteries of God known, and carried a deep burden for the Church of God.

But I suspect the primary source of his agony for these Christians whom he had never met before was his prayer life. His very first word to them in Colossians 1:3 was that "we always pray for you, and we give thanks to God, the Father of our Lord Jesus Christ." Again, in verse 9 he writes, "We have not stopped praying for you since we first heard about you." The Greek word agón appears again in chapter 4 where Paul assures the Colossians that Epaphras "agonizes" in prayer for them just as Paul does. Surely Paul's prayer life for these believers was the primary source of his growing concern for them, for those who pray will find their hearts enlarged, sort of like the heart of Dr. Suess' Grinch that "grew three sizes that day." Prayer has an expansive effect on one's capacity for love, concern, and even suffering for others. As Paul prayed for the Colossians, his mind and heart were aligned with God's and his capacity to agonize over and willingness to suffer for ones he had never even met were expanded.

But what did Paul agonize and struggle *for*? He agonized and struggled that they might know the fullness of Christ.

Chapter 1 begins with Paul's summary of the Colossians' spiritual journey. He recalls how they had received the Good News (Colossians 1:6-7) and how their hope had been fixed upon eternal things (Colossians 1:5) and how they were now living fruitful lives marked by faith and love for all of God's people (Colossians 1:4). But as false teachers began to creep into the church, Paul's prayer in verse 10 was that the Colossians would come to know God better and better and have the patience and endurance they would need to withstand the attacks of the enemy who wants nothing more than for Christians to take their eyes off Jesus.

For Paul, knowing Christ is everything, hence the presence of perhaps the highest Christological passage of the entire New Testament immediately following in Colossians 1:15-20:

Christ is the visible image of the invisible God.

He existed before anything was created and is supreme over all creation,

for through him God created everything
in the heavenly realms and on earth.
He made the things we can see
and the things we can't see —
such as thrones, kingdoms, rulers, and authorities in the
unseen world.

Everything was created through him and for him.

He existed before anything else,
and he holds all creation together.

Christ is also the head of the church,
which is his body.

He is the beginning,
supreme over all who rise from the dead.

So he is first in everything.

For God in all his fullness
was pleased to live in Christ,
and through him God reconciled
everything to himself.

He made peace with everything in heaven and on earth
by means of Christ's blood on the cross.

This is the One he prays they would come to know better and better
(Colossians 1:10). He is not just Jesus, the man, but the One in whom
the whole fullness of deity dwells bodily — the God-man, the One
who is ultimate reality in the flesh revealed, in whom "lie hidden all
the treasures of wisdom and knowledge" (Colossians 2:3). This was
a direct jab at those false teachers claiming a spiritual aristocracy of

enlightenment, whose teachings suggested that knowing Jesus was not enough for salvation. To them, salvation would come from knowing Jesus and something more, to which Paul replies with a resounding, "No." All the treasures of spiritual wisdom and knowledge can be found in Christ and in Christ alone. If you want to know what is ultimately real or lasting or true, you can only find it in him.

The concern of the apostle, the thing he agonized over — an agony born out of the prayerful alignment of his own heart with God's — was that these Christians would know Jesus fully.

How does one come to know Jesus fully? First, it is through the inspired Word of God that is true in all it affirms. One of my greatest joys and satisfactions in leading this church is when a guest comes to one of our worship services and, regardless of who is preaching that particular day tells me afterwards how refreshing it was to hear the Bible preached. Incidentally, this is also a sad commentary on the state of the pulpit in early 21st century American Christianity. For as long as Elizabeth City Evangelical Methodist Church has been present in this corner of northeast North Carolina, we have loved and cherished the Scriptures. We don't elevate the Scriptures as somehow equal to God, but we affirm that they faithfully and truthfully attest to God and alone make Him known in a saving way.

We live in a day when the divine inspiration and reliability and authority of the Bible are under attack perhaps unlike ever before in our nation's history. It is a time when churches, and even whole denominations, seek to recraft it after their own image or abandon it altogether. It is for this reason the Evangelical Methodist Church denomination came into existence in 1946 to begin with, to be a shelter for those who cling to the truth of God's word — men and women, moved by God, who boldly gave up their pulpits, pensions, and properties out of their deep conviction in the Scriptures.

I would contend, after the manner of the apostle himself, that churches today are in need of a renewed desire for teaching that is true rather than teaching that charms. We live in a "2 Timothy 4:3-4" type of day, when fewer and fewer people seek sound and wholesome teaching, but instead follow their own desires and look for teachers who will tell them whatever their itching ears want to hear — rejecting truth and chasing after myths. But to the faithful I say, "Seek those who will rightly divide and preach the Word of God in season or out. Seek those who will speak the truth in love, who will patiently correct, rebuke, and encourage you with right teaching and sound doctrine."

The enduring legacy of this church, that my family and I are blessed to call home, is that for 75 years it has remained committed to the truth of the Word, those sacred writings which are able to make one wise for salvation through faith in Christ Jesus. In a world that is as confused, perverted, rebellious, and deceived as any of us have ever seen in our lifetimes, this church stands firm. We defend the Word, but don't make excuses for it. We don't worship the Word, but we stake our very lives upon it. The founder of our church, George Winslow, once prayed, "Lord, if this church ceases to preach the gospel, let it fail." He didn't mean a half gospel or some partial gospel. He meant the full gospel, the Good News of Jesus Christ toward which both the Old and New Testaments point.

As followers of Jesus living in the blessing of the faithfulness of those gone before us, we affirm on this historic 75th anniversary milestone of our church's life our commitment to the Scriptures and the vision of our founder. We will preach, proclaim, and live out the truth of Christ crucified — a stumbling block to the Jew and foolishness to the Gentile, but to those called by God to salvation,

Christ the power and wisdom and mystery and revelation of the Triune God! He is the One in whom we live and move and have our being, our very life and breath. He is salvation itself, and His Word is true.

Paul wanted the Colossian church to have "complete confidence that they understand God's mysterious plan, which is Christ himself" (Colossians 2:2). While this understanding begins with trusting obedience to the truth of the Scriptures — and there is indeed an intellectual base to knowing Christ — it is incomplete apart from the loving community of the Church. Note the interplay of truth and love at work in the apostle's message. On one hand, the truth of who Christ is forms the basis for real Christian unity. For Paul, the most certain result of the Colossians accepting any new teaching would be the breakdown of their fellowship, which was a consistent concern throughout the New Testament. John, in his first epistle writing to Christians dealing with false teaching, wrote,

> "We proclaim to you the one who existed from the beginning, whom we have heard and seen. We saw him with our own eyes and touched him with our own hands. He is the Word of life. This one who is life itself was revealed to us, and we have seen him. And now we testify and proclaim to you that he is the one who is eternal life. He was with the Father, and then he was revealed to us. We proclaim to you what we ourselves have actually seen and heard." (1 John 1:1-3a)

Why? "So that you may have fellowship with us. And our fellowship is with the Father and with his Son, Jesus Christ. We are writing these things so that you may fully share our joy" (1 John 1:3b-4). John's point was Paul's concern. Jesus is the very substance of Christian fellowship. Miss Him and the fellowship ceases to exist. He holds Creation together; He holds the Body together. He is sustainer of the cosmos; He is sustainer of the Church. Without the Head, the Body does not survive.

On the other hand, the full assurance of the truth about Christ is not attained through intellectual processes alone, but through the Church's corporate life. I think perhaps the New International Version's rendering of Colossians 2:2-3 says it best: "My goal is that they may be encouraged in heart and united in love, so that they may have the full riches of complete understanding, in order that they may know the mystery of God, namely, Christ, in whom are hidden all the treasures of wisdom and knowledge." In other words, the full revelation of God in Christ cannot be properly known or experienced apart from the community of faith. Why is that?

It is in the community of believers where the Holy Love of God is enfleshed. By the presence and power of the Holy Spirit, the Church is the very Body of Christ, and when we are loved by the Church, our knowledge of Jesus is enhanced. When holy love fills and marks a people, they become the face and voice and touch of the Holy One Himself in time and space. It is not theoretical love, or love in the abstract, but holy love at work in and through persons. Allow me to illustrate this.

My family and I experienced the full wrath of COVID-19 in August as the dangerous Delta variant was running rampant. My wife, Rebecca, and I got the worst of it among the five of us. Days of fever, extreme body aches and pains, and sleepless nights were followed by more days of chest pain and difficulty breathing. While neither of us required hospitalization, I can't remember ever being as sick as we were for that week and a half. There was something about the shortness of breath we experienced that caused us both to face our own mortality in ways unlike ever before. The physical toll was matched, and at times surpassed, by the mental and emotional toll from being acutely aware that each labored breath could very well be our last.

One day, toward the end of our bout with the illness, I found Rebecca alone weeping in our bedroom. I assumed she was just overcome by how miserable we all were or from the effects of quarantine on our family life, but I was wrong. She was crying tears of *joy* from the overwhelming expression of God's love through the many people who wrote us cards, fixed us meals, or went out of their way to bring us groceries or medicines or even treats for our kids. These tangible expressions of God's own loving care and concern for our family had moved her deeply.

Those weeks of illness were exceedingly hard on us, but in retrospect we consider them blessed, because through the outreach of our own church family we have come to know yet another dimension of Jesus' own heart and self-giving love toward us. Through ordinary people filled with the very love and life of an extraordinary God, the truths we place our faith in have been verified and confirmed as more than mere propositional truth, but His own glorious Person with and for us. We have been reminded in a fresh new way that the words "real love" and "real life" adorning our church sign are more than a slogan. They are apt descriptions of everything the Body of Christ is to be and do.

All this happens when we are loved by the Body of Christ, but it also happens when we are the ones loving others. When our own hearts are enlarged and we become the very channels of God's grace, we come to know the truth of Christ from personal experience. As God sheds

His very holy love abroad in us, we come to know and experience the mystery of triune life — divine Persons in and for the other. We come to know Jesus better through both the receiving *and* the giving of love, for it is through intimate relationship with the Body that we attain the full knowledge of Christ. What an astounding mystery, and yet the greatest joy in life: To be in Him, together, with you!

Friends, the Apostle Paul did not believe in the inevitability of perseverance. He was keenly aware of the efforts of the enemy to invade the flock and the possibility that sheep might be led astray. He knew and warned believers about the dangers of being "captured by empty philosophies and high-sounding nonsense that come from human thinking and from the spiritual powers of this world, rather than from Christ" (Colossians 2:8). But if you study the Scriptures with all your mind and love Christ and His Body with all your heart, you can stand firm with unbroken ranks against the pressures of the world, the flesh, and the devil, shoulder to shoulder with your brothers and sisters, together with eyes fixed on Jesus. Then "you will be strengthened with all his glorious power so you will have all the endurance and patience you need" (Colossians 1:11). By God's grace, this is what the Church has always been, and this is what it will continue to be until He returns or calls us home.

"And now, just as you accepted Christ Jesus as your Lord, you must continue to follow him. Let your roots grow down into him, and let your lives be built on him. Then your faith will grow strong in the truth you were taught, and you will overflow with thankfulness." (Colossians 2:6-7)

Reverend Sean Scribner is the lead pastor at Elizabeth City Evangelical Methodist Church in Elizabeth City, NC. A native of central Ohio, Pastor

Sean and his family moved to North Carolina in October of 2013 to come on staff at EMC in the role of Associate Pastor. He moved into the role of Lead Pastor in 2017.

In 2003 he married an amazing Mississippi woman named Rebecca and together they have three precious children: Savannah, Nathan, and William. In 2004 he earned his B.A. in Christian Ministries from Ohio Christian University in Circleville, OH and in 2008 he earned his M.A. in Theology from Wesley Biblical Seminary in Jackson, MS. Sean's deep conviction is that the local church is the center of God's purposes in the world and he desires nothing more greatly than to be a part of people coming to know, love, and follow Jesus.

CHAPTER SEVEN

Holy Love and Discipleship

Nathan Doyle

Tribute

I first met Dr. Bill Ury in the fall of 2000 when I enrolled at Wesley Biblical Seminary and jumped right into his systematic theology course on day one. From the very beginning every time I heard him teach or preach God increasingly captured my mind and heart through his ministry. I not only loved what he taught but how he taught — as one clearly consumed by holy love. I took every one of his classes I possibly could and have continued to seek out his teaching through his podcasts, online lectures or anytime I heard he would be preaching within driving distance (like within 1,000 miles or so). Some fond memories are attached to opportunities I had to serve the

Ury family through housesitting and taking care of their pets while they were away. It was directly related to one of those opportunities that I ended up saddled with 19 puppies and the stray who gave birth to them during my final year of school. When our fourth son was born, my wife and I had decided to name him Uriah but were excited when we realized that instead of the more common spelling of Uri we could spell his nickname Ury, in honor of Bill. I'll always be grateful to God for the grace that He has worked in me through my friend and teacher Dr. Bill Ury.

Essay

What does discipleship have to do with holy love? One describes the nature of God while the other is an invitation into the life of God.

As a pastor over the past 20 years, I've spent a great deal of energy wrestling with the subject of discipleship. Several years ago, I was grateful to be included in a multiple year study of discipleship sponsored by my denomination that culminated with the crafting of a new mission statement that defined us as, "A Group of Churches Who Exist to Make Disciples Who Make Disciples." Throughout much of the process I couldn't elude the gnawing suspicion that we, myself included, were not so much after the deep intimacy that discipleship requires, but something more mechanical. A step-by-step process which would substantiate that someone had passed the appropriate qualifications, whatever those may be, to be called a disciple of Jesus Christ.

Of course, some benchmarks that might border on the mechanical, are necessary for discipleship. Before leaving Earth

Jesus left the church with the instructions to, "Go, therefore, and make disciples of all nations...teaching them to follow all that I commanded you..."[*] In order to teach *everything* that Jesus commanded, and not miss some vital points, there will need to be some type of objective standards that can be used to show advancement in discipleship. Much of what Jesus commanded, however, is so relational in nature that checklists on their own would fail to be sufficient measurements of achievement. It can be difficult, for instance, to standardize the process of learning how to "love one another" or "to bear with one another" let alone how to "be one" as the Father and Son are one, to name just a few examples. The only way to ensure that these commands are accomplished in discipleship is to engage in intimate relationship with others; relationships that will be discomforting and at times messy, yet essential for effective discipleship.

An Invitation into the Triune Life

Discipleship is an invitation to a relationship which far exceeds all other relationships in its potential for intimacy. It is not solely an invitation to a confessional faith comprised of assent to codified statements of belief, though that is one aspect of how discipleship is engaged. Ultimately, discipleship has as its goal Christlikeness which is only possible through a relationship of identification with Jesus. This occurs when disciples respond to God's call to draw near and in the process of coming into proximity to holy love are transformed into His likeness.

Just prior to Jesus beginning His earthly ministry He appeared

---

[*]   Matthew 28:19 NASB

in the wilderness where John, the forerunner to the Messiah, was baptizing people in the Jordan River. John was clear in his preaching that his baptism was for repentance, yet it foreshadowed a deeper experience, the baptism with the Holy Spirit, that Jesus would make available to those belonging to Him.[*] It was a hint to the triune relationship believers are invited into which Jesus would make more explicit in His words to the disciples on the night of His betrayal. In that final sermon, Jesus repeatedly referenced the Holy Spirit as the gift of the Father and Son, who was distinct yet also identified with Him. He said, "I will ask the Father, and He will give you *another* Helper, so that He may be with you forever. The Helper is the Spirit of truth, whom the world cannot receive, because it does not see Him or know Him; but you know Him because He remains with you and will be in you."[†] Jesus was promising intimacy with *Another* yet at the same time was identifying Himself with this *Other*. He followed those words with, "I will not leave you as orphans; I am coming to you," and, "On that day you will know that I am in My Father, and you are in Me, and I in you."[‡] His words reveal that when the Holy Spirit comes, Jesus Himself also comes to dwell in believers.[§]

What does it mean, then, to be "baptized with the Holy Spirit?" It means intimate union with Christ. The Greek word βαπτίζω, which can carry the connotation of something that is "overwhelmed," might be used to indicate the breadth of the transformation implied in such an encounter as uniting with God Himself.[¶] The Scriptural

---

[*] Matthew 3:11 NASB
[†] John 14:16-17 NASB
[‡] John 14:18 & 20 NASB
[§] In several places the Spirit is called "the Spirit of Christ" as in Romans 8:9 and 1 Peter 1:11.
[¶] (Gingrich 1979, 131)

example found in Galatians 3 seems pertinent here, "for all you who were baptized into Christ have clothed yourselves with Christ."* The verb, translated "have clothed yourselves," is derived from a root, δύνω, which means "to be plunged into" or "sink into."† In the New Testament the root is only used when describing the setting sun.‡ This seems an odd root to convey the concept of putting on clothing, for no one 'sinks' into their clothing. Unless it is meant to imply a surpassing experience, as when the sun sinking below the horizon appears to be consumed by it. Putting on Christ, then, is not merely adding something to one's own life, but rather depicts the all-consuming experience of being swallowed up in His life.

The Goal of Face-to-Face

How must discipleship be carried out if it involves immersion into the life of holy love? In a word, it must be incarnational; personal not merely propositional. God in His wisdom has so designed this process as to require a human person with a face to get in front of as an extension of His own face. This is ultimately what God is after, face-to-face relationships with His creatures. It can be seen from the opening pages of Scripture as God forms the first human out of dust and, "breathed into his nostrils the breath of life."§ The first instance of CPR in the history of the world is between God and Adam. I know just enough of modern CPR to know the proper procedure is to tip the head back, pinch the nose and breath into the mouth. This is the most efficient way to force air into another's

---

* Galatians 3;27 NASB
† (Gingrich 1979, 209)
‡ As in Mark 1:32 and Luke 4:40
§ Genesis 2:7

87

lungs. I'm intrigued, however, by the wording of the Scripture which describes God blowing into Adam's "nostrils." Was God unaware of the proper way to perform CPR? Of course not! The way God chose, while maybe not the most efficient, is by far the most personal. One does not breathe into another's nostrils without getting face-to-face.*

This kind of intimacy is what God intended for humanity from the outset, so it is no surprise that it is hinted at all throughout Scripture. Several months ago, out of curiosity, I decided to look up the most frequently used words in the Old Testament. The list of the first 20 words consists primarily of minor connecting words such as: and, to, for, with, from, whom, etc.† Moving on to the next 20 words I was surprised to find the Hebrew word for face, פָּנִים, as the 26th most used word in the Old Testament occurring well over 2,000 times.‡ This word is so prevalent in Scripture because it beautifully captures the type of relationship God desires with people, face-to-face.

As an example, in Exodus, as God sought to establish a new relationship with Israel, He offered many invitations to intimacy, sometimes through the introduction of difficult circumstances. He made encountering difficulty part of the journey to show them firsthand His providential care. On one occasion while the people grumbled in their hunger, God provided meat in the form of quail covering the camp each evening. Before the quail arrive, however,

---

* It is also interesting that the breath of "life" God breathed into Adam is in the plural, "breath of lives." Hinting of the Trinity, as more than just one life is breathed into Adam. An invitation to holy love that God offered Adam and holds out to all humanity hidden within the text.

† Not entirely inconsequential as most of these words are relational themselves in the sense that they are referential or connecting words that only appear in relation to other words.

‡ This word can also refer to the personal presence of another. (Holladay 1988, 293-294)

Moses instructs Aaron to tell the people to, "come near before the Lord, for He has heard your grumblings."[*] The word Moses instructs Aaron to use, יִנָּפֵל, is a cognate of *panim*, the Hebrew for face, thus this instruction could be understood as a call to "approach the face" of God. The grumbling of the people represented a relational problem to which the solution was to come face-to-face with God.

One of my favorite metaphors in the Old Testament is found in the phrase "apple of my eye." It so poignantly captures the kind of intimacy God is after with humanity.[†] The phrase "apple of my eye" was one I remember my grandmother using but I never really understood it. Much later in life I learned that it originated from Scripture and was formed from the Hebrew עַיִן, meaning 'eye' and אִישׁוֹן, often translated as "pupil." What really makes the phrase helpful, though, is the fact that אִישׁוֹן is the diminutive of the Hebrew word for man. Diminutives are additions to a root word that change the meaning to a smaller version of the root. As in Spanish 'casa' means house and 'casita' means little house. So, the phrase "apple of His eye" literally means disciples are to be the "little man" in His eye. What this describes is that God wants us to live in such an intimate face-to-face orientation to Him that might enable us to see our reflection in His pupil.

The problem, of course, is sin and particularly the shame which accompanies sin. One can imagine the scene in the garden after the first sin, as Adam and Eve hear God walking in the garden but instead

---

[*] Exodus 16:9 NASB

[†] The phrase "apple of the eye" shows up a couple times in possibly the most personal book of Scripture, as in Psalm 17:7-8, "Show Your wonderful faithfulness Savior of those who take refuge at Your right hand...keep me as the apple of the eye." It also occurs in Deuteronomy where God is describing His people metaphorically through Jacob, "He found him in a desert land...He encircled him, He cared for him, He guarded him as the apple of His eye." (Deuteronomy 32:9-10).

of running to greet Him (face-to-face) they are found hiding in the bushes. God calls to them, "Where are you?" He calls not because He didn't know their whereabouts but for their benefit so they might realize the gravity of their situation. Instead of enjoying the intimacy with God for which they were created, they now experience separation. The Scriptures do not indicate whether Adam ever came out from hiding. It's possible the whole ensuing conversation happened from a distance. Yet if Adam ever did emerge, I imagine he did so with his face glued to the ground unable to make eye contact with God.

God provided a poignant illustration of this recently through an encounter with my youngest son, Levi. As a one-year-old he was at the age where frequent correction was needed, yet I wasn't sure how much he understood either his error or the ensuing discipline. The solution I arrived at was to have him hold my gaze while I tried to reason with him, as much as one can with a one-year-old, about what was wrong with his actions. Early on he had no problem managing extended eye contact when I would say, "Levi, look at me." The day he refused to look at me, and his little lip came out in a pout while his chin remained glued to his chest, it was then I realized he understood. The awareness of wrongdoing had broken the innocent intimacy we enjoyed, and shame took its place.

Face-to-Face Discipleship

How can discipleship accomplish reorienting us into a face-to-face relationship with holy love? Well, until Jesus returns, and He is seen literally face-to-face, God has set it up to happen through His incarnation in the Church. Through personal discipling relationships willing to take the risks and endure the discomfort of intimacy.

The principle of incarnation is what has historically set apart the Wesleyan model of society, class and band. Specifically, the radical intimacy of the band meetings which required the accountability of another. Participants, to gain admittance, agreed to, "speak each of us in order, freely and plainly, the true state of our souls."* As Thomas Oden described it, "This process was not for the faint of heart or for those who wanted to sit back and observe. It was profoundly participatory from the outset…Every participant was expected to listen and contribute from the heart to the hearts of others…Describing participants' relationship with God in the present was the central concern of the conversation."†

This describes a very incarnational discipleship scenario where the members of the group extend the intimate presence of God toward one another. Wesley prescribed very searching and personal questions to be asked of each disciple including: "What known sins have you committed since our last meeting?" or "What temptations have you met with?"‡

In fact, communication that promoted intimacy was the primary purpose of the bands. There is no mention of the use of Scriptures prescribed in the "Rules of the Band Societies" Wesley drew up on December 25, 1738. A close examination of the rules themselves reveals Wesley's main concern was not Bible study but a focus on testimony which included: confession, praise and thanksgiving. In modern usage, however, when the class model has not been as effective, the failure can most likely be traced back to a short-circuiting of the questions and testimonies that promote intimacy.

---

* (Wesley 2002, Vol 8 pg 272)
† (Oden 2014, 30-31)
‡ (Wesley 2002, Vol 8 pg 273)

Shame is a powerful impediment to intimacy and can cause a reluctance to face the harder questions. It is often apparent in the body language of group participants by, among other clues, diverting one's eyes. The "apple of my eye" metaphor can be illustrative in this regard. It can be incredibly discomforting how close a person must get to another's face before seeing their reflection in the pupil. Try it sometime. Yet this is the level of intimacy that God is after. This raises a serious question for discipleship: If disciples are not willing to be face-to-face with one another around the grace of transformation, how will they ever stand face-to-face with holy love? God has commanded us to make disciples of others as a practice in intimacy so that we can learn to be intimate with Him and ultimately be ready to stand before Him face-to-face when He returns. The effectiveness of discipleship will be proportionate to the willingness of the disciples to welcome intimacy.

Nothing can short-circuit the intimacy of discipleship like a lack of surrender to self-giving by the participants. This is true not just for the disciples but especially the one doing the discipling, for a person cannot lead others to a place where they have not been led. It is a common mistake of leaders to think they must be so above reproach that they resist the transparency and the humility of self-giving. Yet this is the nature of holy love to always be humbly and openly moving toward another, expressed most clearly in the incarnation. As Paul writes, "Have this attitude in yourselves which was also in Christ Jesus, who, as He already existed in the form of God, did not consider equality with God something to be grasped, but emptied Himself by taking the form of a bondservant...."* If anyone could be above reproach it would be Jesus, and yet He was

---

* Philippians 2:5-7 NASB

willing to be identified with humanity. Tempted in the same ways as humans. Subjected to the same limitations and struggles. All to be face-to-face with people. Incarnational leaders are not afraid to be the first to testify, confess and identify with the ones they lead. It is no coincidence that John Wesley was so successful in developing bands that brought about tremendous transformation for he spent many years himself as a member of a 'holy club' that contributed to his own transformation. To make disciples one must be a disciple.

David modelled this openness in Psalm 51 when he cried out, "Do not cast me away from Your presence."* Coincidentally, the word he uses is מִיָּנֶ, which could be understood, "Don't send me away from Your face." Instead of separation, he asks God to restore the "joy of His salvation" and to sustain him with a "willing spirit." It is *after* David is willing to be intimately transparent and led by God Himself into a discipling relationship that he can in turn lead others, "Then I will teach wrongdoers Your ways, and sinners will be converted to You."† Leaders enjoying increasing intimacy with God and calling others to the same experience is the heartbeat of discipleship.

Modern discipleship is often reduced to the transfer of information *about* God, but what the Church really needs to wrestle with is how to transmit intimacy *with* God. While knowing God requires knowing some information about Him, it is my conviction that where there is little interest or promotion of the personal presence of God there will soon be a dearth of interest for those propositions about God. The life of the church is at stake and the sanctifying reality of intimacy with God for all who belong to her.

---

*   Psalm 51:11
†   Psalm 51:13

Nathan Doyle is husband to Heather and father to six children: Isaiah, Moriah, Ezekiel, Uriah, Elijah and Levi. He has pastored the multi-site Venture Church with campuses in Youngstown and Streetsboro, Ohio for the past 18 years. He is a lifelong Primitive Methodist and serves as a faculty member of the PM School of Theology and Superintendent of the Pittsburgh District. He holds a bachelor's degree in history from Huntington University and a M.Div. as well as D.Min. from Wesley Biblical Seminary.

CHAPTER EIGHT

Holy Love and Mission to the Least

Bill Dunigan

Tribute

The soul of man is an exceedingly precious thing. Although it's an eternal thing it is also fragile and delicate and requires nurturing and love to become a thing of beauty, a work of art that lifts the souls of others. The soul arrives in this world in the form of a newborn child. The parents are first entrusted with the sacred responsibility of imprinting upon this soul love, belonging, security, trust, and a sense of wonder. The soul of M. William Ury was placed in the trembling hands of his parents. I am confident that they immediately dedicated that newborn soul to the one holy God whom they loved and served and then began to lovingly and expertly shape that soul into a man of God and a man for the world. This work, the shaping of Bill and his siblings, would be their greatest work.

My soul became intertwined with Bill's in the early fall of 1974 on the day we both arrived at Asbury College. Bill and I were roommates for four years and have remained brothers ever since. During those four years I watched the soul of this man of God continue to take shape, imprinted by college professors, chapel speakers, coaches, and friends. Bill had, and still has, a voracious appetite for knowledge, and he devoured it constantly. He also had and still has a passionate love for God and His Word. These appetites and passions have further nourished and shaped his soul. As our two souls came together like iron sharpening iron my own soul benefited greatly.

Over the years I have seen the soul of this man of God become a thing of winsome beauty, a true work of art that continues to lift the souls of more than he will ever know.

Essay

"And the king will answer them, 'Truly I tell you,
just as you did it to one of the least of these
who are members of my family, you did it to me.'"
Matthew 25:40 NRSV

We all want to be counted among those spoken of in this passage. Those who have fed the hungry, given water to the thirsty, welcomed the stranger, clothed the naked, and visited the sick or imprisoned. Serving the least is equivalent to serving Jesus Himself. If we truly desire to serve the least, we will want to do it in a way that would please Jesus. The truth is that even when the need seems obvious, as in the examples given in this passage, there are times when our attempts to help others are misguided or aren't received in the way we envisioned. I remember a story, related to me by Bill Ury some time ago. It happened when he was a student at The Institute of Holy Land Studies in Jerusalem. As I remember it, there was a group of tourists loading onto a bus. One of the tourists saw a person who appeared to be in need. When they attempted to give the person a donation the tour guide snatched the money from their hand exclaiming, "I will not allow you to turn my people into a nation of beggars!"

How do we help the least in the right way? How do we help without doing harm? A key is found in considering the position we are coming from, the posture we take when serving the least. We want our mission to the least to be guided by the holy love of God. We want our service to the least to be pleasing to Jesus. How then does holy love act toward the least? What posture does holy love take? To answer these questions, we must look to Jesus, our flesh and blood example of holy love.

One common posture taken when we want to help is what I will call the posture of "offering a hand." When acting from this posture we *reach down* to offer a hand to someone who is perceived to be, if even for the moment, on a lower plane. The posture of offering a hand is not always the wrong one. It is often just what is needed and at times we offer a hand simply because we are the ones still on our feet. Picture the ball player who has taken a fall and a teammate offers them a hand or reaching out to help a community after a natural disaster. If the help comes from someone who is *looking down on* the one to whom they are offering a hand, however, that person can suffer a loss of dignity no matter the intentions of the giver.

It is simply a fact of life in this world that we do not always stand on the same plane. Those of us who are in fact more fortunate, who have had more advantages, or have had the privilege of better education or better paying jobs can find it difficult to help others in ways that don't also hurt them.

When I was ministering in Boston, a mission team came to do work in our community. A woman from our congregation had a neighbor, an elderly shut-in, whose yard needed work. I took the team to her house where they worked to clean up the yard that had not received attention for quite some time. The house had a hedge in the front that was very overgrown and spindly. Having worked as a landscaper while in high school and college, I knew that in for the hedge to become fuller, it needed to be cut down to a foot or so in height. We did just that. Later I received a call from our parishioner informing me that her neighbor was terribly upset when she saw what we had done to her hedge. As it turned out the elderly lady suffered from anthropophobia, she feared other people; the hedge had helped her to feel protected and we had destroyed that protection. I was trying to help, but I did it wrong. I operated from my position of having superior knowledge and experience, regarding hedges at least. I in fact did more harm than good. I violated a cardinal principle that I will detail later. I did not display holy love and Jesus was likely as displeased as the now terrified shut-in.

Another posture that has gained popularity in our time, meant to restore more dignity to the one being helped, is the posture of "coming alongside." Here we strive to place ourselves on the same plane as the ones we desire to help. We pull on our gloves and work side-by-side with those in need. It is good that we have more and more people willing to take this posture, but it too is not without pitfalls. It is sometimes not clear, in the perception of those being helped, as to whether we are coming alongside them or coming *down* to their neighborhood.

There is a third posture, the posture of holy love taken by Jesus. It is the posture of "going under," taking the position or posture of a servant, taking the attitude of humility, emptying one's heart of pride and selfishness, and replacing those things with love for God and for His creation, especially the least.

Jesus chose to go under. He did not reach down from heaven to pull us up, and although at first glance it may look like He came alongside, upon further examination it will be seen that He assumed the lowest position possible.

The lowly position taken by Jesus is first seen in His Incarnation *of*. Galatians 4:4 states, "But when the fullness of time had come, God sent his Son, born a woman . . .." God had determined that time had reached its fullness, was complete or filled up. Now God was going to intervene in a very direct way. Now He would send His Son to show us just how a life of fellowship and obedience, a life of holy love, should be lived.

God took on our very flesh and blood, born in the exact way we are born. The infinite God became a single cell, and joining that cell with a human cell, the life of the incarnate Jesus began. The Son of God took on the lowest form of human life possible. From that instant, His growth and development, indeed His very life was derived from blood flowing through the veins of a woman. A woman of no means or consequence, betrothed to a common tradesman.

We should not make the mistake of thinking that the place of His birth was a mere happenstance that adds romance to His story or is meant to emphasizes the heartlessness of the occupying Roman nation. The sovereign God had preordained that Messiah would be born in Bethlehem and He chose the lowliest delivery room available. Not the clean and sterile environment to which we are accustomed, but one smeared with manure, filled with flies, and the stench of beasts of burden. If there is tragedy in the circumstances surrounding His birth, it is tragedy of the sort common to many throughout history, the tragedy of the common man. No, the tragedy of the least, and Jesus, God's only Son, became the least.

Jesus began as one of the least and He maintained that position, that posture, throughout His life on earth. Jesus' identification with the lowly cannot be denied. He was homeless, having no place to lay His head (Matthew 8:20), depended upon the generosity of others and taught His followers to do the same (Matthew 10:9-11). He died like a criminal (Matthew 26:50 and following). He urged His listeners to "consider the ravens and the lilies" (Luke 12:24,27) not worrying about food or clothing. He knew hunger (Mark 11:12), and weariness (John 4:6), and was no stranger to discomfort. Sleeping on the ground was something to which Jesus and His followers must have grown accustomed as they traveled from place to place or spent time in the wilderness.

This posture taken by Jesus stood out in stark contrast to the posture of the religious leaders of that time who understood God's holiness but not His love. The pride of the Pharisees (separatists) was well known. Jesus told a parable of one who thanked God that he was not as other men (Luke 18:10-14). Jesus had harsh words for the scribes. He condemned them for laying heavy burdens of religious laws upon the people, for doing their works to be seen by others, for their religious show and their love of honor, calling them whitewashed tombs (Matthew 23:2-33).

The contrast between the attitude of Jesus and that of the religious leaders is seen clearly in the conversation Jesus has with an expert in the Mosaic law who is attempting to assert his own superior religiosity (Luke 10:29-37). Jesus tells the lawyer a story about a man traveling from Jerusalem to Jericho who falls into the hands of robbers who strip him, beat him, and leave him half dead. A priest and then a Levite see the man, but each goes out of their way to avoid him as they pass by. The story so far would not have surprised the lawyer. A priest would give this man a wide berth as encountering what might be a dead body would defile him (Leviticus 21:1-3) and would require ritual cleansing lasting seven days (Numbers 19:2-13; Ezekiel 44:24-27). The Levite might have avoided the robbery victim as well, just for good measure. But Jesus goes on. Next comes a Samaritan, a member of a lowly class of half-breed persons whom the Jews despised. This Samaritan, moved by compassion rather than religious compulsion, shockingly cares for the fallen man at a significant cost to himself. The Samaritan displayed love for his neighbor, fulfilling by his actions the admonition of the second greatest commandment which the lawyer claimed to religiously uphold. The lawyer offers no rebuttal. The actions of the priest and even the Levite were not seen by him as unusual but rather what one would expect. Perhaps he would have done the same.

Jesus' own actions were often even more shocking. He did not behave in a manner that had come to be expected of a religious leader. Jesus was approachable. He was not above communing with even the most despised and rejected. A matter which caused the respected religious leaders to despise and reject Him outright. Jesus ministered to, even touching, the outcast lepers (Matthew 8:2). Jesus welcomed and refused to condemn women, children, tax collectors, prostitutes, the woman caught in adultery, sinners, and thieves. A woman who had suffered from hemorrhages for twelve years, a condition which would have made her "unclean" (Leviticus 15:25-27) felt that she could not outwardly approach Jesus. Hidden within the covering of the crowd she came near and touching His cloak was immediately healed. Jesus, however, would not let it go at that. He sought her out. Then without condemning her for her violation, He commended her faith and bade her to go in peace.

When a blind beggar outside of the town of Jericho cried out to Jesus, he was sternly ordered by those around him to be quiet. Ignoring their appeal to respectability he called out even more loudly. At this Jesus called the man to come to Him. The beggar made a hasty path to stood before Jesus who then did something inexplicable. He said to the blind beggar, "What do you want Me to do for you?" Had I been in that crowd I would have wondered about the eyesight or perhaps the judgment of Jesus. The man was blind! Was there any doubt that he wanted Jesus to restore his sight? Yet Jesus asks. This is a startling example of the servant posture of Jesus. A person taking the posture of lending a hand or even coming along side, will often assume that they know what the other person needs without asking. It is an easy thing, a natural thing to think that due to my education or background or position I am a better judge of someone's needs. Especially if I see that person as inferior to me in education, background, experience, or position. Remember my story of the hedge? Yet Jesus, always the servant, did not act until He received direction from the blind beggar!

The holy love of God dwelling within the heart of Jesus compelled Him not to consider Himself greater than any other man, even those whom others considered the least. Jesus in fact assumed the role of a bond servant, a slave. Philippians 2;6,7 states; "though he was in the form of God, did not regard equality with

God as something to be exploited, (ἁρπαγμὸν) (grasped, claimed, seized, plundered, held fast, retained) but emptied himself, taking the form of a slave, being born in human likeness". Jesus did not try to hold on to or retain His equality with God, but relinquishing that claim, He accepted the position of slave.

John 13:2-17 tells us that "Jesus, knowing that the Father had given all things into his hands, and that he had come from God and was going to God, got up from the table, took off his outer robe, and tied a towel around himself." After clothing Himself as a servant, He then preformed the servant's chore of washing the feet of the dinner guests. This act was done as a very clear example, to teach a very clear lesson. Jesus, to make sure that His disciples understand the lesson, asked them, "Do you know what I have done for you?" Without waiting for their answer, He clarified everyone's position. "You call me Teacher and Lord — and you are right, for that is what I am. So if I, your Lord and Teacher have washed your feet, (became your servant) you also ought to wash one another's feet (become servants to one another). For I have set you an example, that you should do as I have done to you."

Notice the part about Jesus knowing that the Father had given all things into His hands, had given Him all authority, and that He had come from God and was going to God. Jesus knew that His position with God the Father could not be shaken. Again, it was something He did not need to grasp at, seize or plunder (Philippians 2:6). He knew where He stood with God the Father. He did not need the esteem of man because He had intimacy with the Father. In modern vernacular we would say His self-esteem was intact. This gave Jesus the solid footing that allowed Him to empty Himself and become a servant.

Since our Fall, having lost intimacy and the security of our position with the Father we tend to grasp at and seize anything that will restore our self-esteem, even plundering it from others when we can. We are lacking, so we are always grasping, always holding fast, for we are ever aware of our loss. We find it extremely difficult if not impossible, to surrender any esteem we have managed to claim in this world. To empty ourselves and take the form of a servant, a slave, is beyond our human ability. If we are to have the kind of love for the least that Jesus had, it must be holy love. It must be imparted to us as a gift of holiness. It must come from God. It must flow through us from the indwelling presence of Christ Jesus by the power of the Holy Spirit.

Singer songwriter Rich Mullins was living on a Navajo reservation teaching music to the children there. He served there without compensation. He lived on a salary which he drew from the royalties of his many records. But he insisted that his salary should be consistent with the amount made by the average laborer in the U.S., and he donated the rest of his income to charities. In the late summer of 1997, Rich sat down in an old, abandoned church and with a cassette tape player recorded demos for what would end up being his last album. A collection of songs about Jesus, that cassette tape would be the only recording of those songs ever made by Rich himself. He died in a car crash shortly thereafter.[*] One of the songs on that tape begins with these words:

> We didn't know what love was 'til He came
> And He gave love a face and He gave love a name[†]

The holy love of God, given a face and a name by Jesus can live

---

[*]   Lou Carlozo, *Rich Mullins' Last Musical Vision* (Chicago Tribune, June 28, 1998).
[†]   Rich Mullins, *All the Way to Kingdom Come* (The Jesus Record, 1998).

within and should rule the hearts of His followers. Many across the centuries have been compelled by that holy love to serve and to love the least. They have embraced the posture of "going under," the servant posture. Those who have taken the lowest posture in life, although it is a thing they would have never sought or even accepted, are highly honored for their service to Christ through their service to the least. They stood out in their humility and service as examples of the posture of holy love. They have often come along at times when the Church stood in need of what we would today call an "attitude adjustment." Just as in the time of the advent of Christ, the people of God have too often become self-serving, turning their backs upon, or creating barriers for, the least among us. Perhaps the Spirit of Jesus is calling you and me to go under, to become servants, for the sake of His Church in our time.

William (Bill) Dunigan is a retired officer in The Salvation Army, after 36 years of service. He and his wife Sue served for 22 of those years in incarnational urban ministry, living in the inner-city neighborhoods of Dorchester in Boston and Camden, New Jersey. Over the years, he and Sue raised three children and took hundreds of college students and others who God brought to them into their home and family. Bill's ministry focused on disciple making and service to the least, through the gift of hospitality.

Bill Dunigan is a graduate of Asbury College where he received a BA in Psychology, Asbury Theological Seminary earning an MAR in Christian Education and Evangelism, and The Salvation Army School for Officer's Training in Suffern New York. After retirement Bill fulfilled a lifelong dream of Thru Hiking the 2,200 miles of the Appalachian Trail.

CHAPTER NINE

Holy Love and
The Ivory Tower

W. David Buschart

Tribute

My years of doctoral studies at Drew University were blessed with the fellowship of a wonderful cadre of colleagues. Though my path does not cross Bill's (and Diane's) nearly as frequently as I (and my wife, Nancy) would like, it is a testimony to how rich, while also daunting for all of us those years were, and to Bill and Di's faithfulness.

I referred above to enjoying a wonderful cadre of colleagues during doctoral studies at Drew. While ecclesiastical identities do not reveal all or even the most important facets of a person, the ecclesiastical "homes" of the members of this group of want-to-be theological scholars gives a sense of the kind of diversity that characterized our shared experiences: Free Church, Presbyterian, Christian and Missionary Alliance, Lutheran, Wesleyan, and Methodist. As he was in all contexts, Bill was a shining light amid this group. Listening to what others had to say. Smiling. Laughing. Asking good questions. Sometimes questions to deepen his own understanding. Sometimes questions intended to prompt the recipient to perhaps consider thinking differently. Always a good word about Jesus. And when the discussion was over there was often an arm around the shoulder accompanied by a kind or encouraging word.

Nancy and I had been married about two years when we arrived at Drew. Bill was single. But before too long he began to talk, frequently, about "Diane." It was clear that something — or more accurately, someone — was up. We enjoyed many dinners together in our tiny, roach-occupied student apartment. Bill is a wise discerner of persons, so it is not surprising that over these dinners he often sought Nancy's listening-ear and wisdom regarding his courtship with Diane. What a gift it was to witness their wedding. The rest is beautiful history.

Essay

"Is there a way of conceiving of love which
will rescue it from its moral exile and
make it a useful guide in recovering 'holiness'
from its ivory-tower irrelevance?"
Mildred Bangs Wynkoop, *A Theology of Love**

---

* Mildred Bangs Wynkoop, A Theology of Love: The Dynamic of Wesleyanism (Kansas

"We love because he first loved us."
1 John 4:19

". . . it is not the mind alone that thinks, but the man."
A. G. Sertillanges, *The Intellectual Life**

Introduction

We live in a time of cultural upheaval. At present very few, if any, sectors of society or institutional arenas are not approached with a hermeneutic of suspicion. Higher education, sometimes referred to as "the academy," is by no means immune to such critique about everything from inflated costs and harmful curricula, to racism and misogyny, from the financial oppression of non-faculty employees to corruption in admissions. Important as these issues *de jour* are, this essay seeks to engage some longer-standing and more deeply rooted perceptions and critiques of the academy and the people engaged most directly in its work — faculty and students. These critiques are often expressed — whether explicitly or implicitly — in the phrase "the Ivory Tower."

One sees this, for example, in Mildred Bangs Wynkoop's adjectival rendering, referring to the "ivory-tower irrelevance" to which holiness has been subjected.[†] The metaphor "ivory tower" began to be applied to academic institutions in the nineteenth century, and over the course of the 1930s-1940s "it became a common phrase attached to universities . . . [and] it became a way

---

City, MO: Beacon Hill Press, 1972), 10.
* A. G. Sertillanges, The Intellectual Life: Its Spirit, Conditions, Methods, trans. Mary Ryan, foreword by James V. Schall (Washington, DC: Catholic University of America Press, 1998), 20.
† Wynkoop, *Theology of Love*, 10.

of criticizing practices and institutions deemed to be 'irrelevant'."*
In addition to viewing academic work as an exercise in irrelevance,
those who carry out such work, both professors and students, are
often regarded as occupying a space which is somehow apart from
"the real world." While it is clearly beyond the scope this brief
essay to address all the misunderstandings and stereotypes (as well
as accurate understandings) which undergird notions of "the Ivory
Tower" and "the real world," we can suggest a different, and more
appropriate, conceptual approach to the academy and academic
work, an approach which is congruent with the reality of holy love.

Toward this end the essay will proceed in two parts, with
two dimensions woven throughout. The first part will reflect in a
general way upon the relationship between holy love and the so-
called "Ivory Tower." This will be followed by some reflections on
two major components of academic work: the pursuit of knowledge
and the sharing of the fruit of that pursuit. Interspersed throughout
both parts will be a mixture of description, depicting something of
the people and work of the academy, and aspiration, envisioning
the way the people and work of academy can and should be. In
a manner somewhat analogous to the realization of holiness in
our world, the descriptive and the aspirational will be interwoven,
being sometimes explicit while at other times being implicit.

---

* Steven Shapin, "The Ivory Tower: The History of a Figure of Speech and Its Cultural
Uses," in *The British Journal for the History of Science* 45(1): 1. http://nrs.harvard.edu/urn-
3:HUL.InstRepos:8336536 (accessed January 21, 2022).

Holy Love and "The Ivory Tower"

Among the many divine attributes is the omnipresence of God. This real presence is poignantly depicted in the rhetorical questions of Psalm 139: "Where can I go from your Spirit? Where can I flee from your presence?" (v. 7). God is utterly free to be where He wishes to be in whatever fashion He wishes to be. No person, no force, no thing can thwart God from being wherever and however He chooses to be. In the context of the new covenant those who are following Jesus are assured by Him, "surely I am with you always, to the very end of the age" (Matthew 28:20). While this promise clearly has a chronological, forward-looking orientation it also carries the "geographical" and circumstantial assurance of His presence wherever His followers go. God's omnipresence is part of what the Apostle Paul seeks to unveil for the Athenians when he cites one of their poets saying, "in him we live and move and have our being" (Acts 17:28).

The wonder of God's omnipresence is accompanied by the marvel of His immanence. God is not simply "there" but is engaged in and with the world. Even as He is exalted in His transcendence, the Son through whom all was created is now "sustaining all things by his powerful word" (Hebrews 1:3). God is present and active in the world. And He is not present and active only in the created order, or in some merely "objective" fashion. He is present in the most personal way and ways. He is present to all people. Again, recalling Paul's proclamations in Athens, God "himself gives everyone life and breath and everything else" and he, Paul, prompts his hearers to "seek him and perhaps reach out for him and find him" (Acts 17:25, 27). Scott Duvall and Daniel Hays have presented a strong case that the "*relational* presence of God" constitutes "the cohesive center" of the Bible.* God is not simply "there" nor is He simply "here." God is personally, relationally present, lovingly working the good of Creation in general and the good of humankind in particular.

Who is this God who is omnipresent, immanent, relationally present to this world and to the people in it? On the one hand, this God is beyond description. Those of the Orthodox Christian tradition know perhaps better than many of us that human thoughts and words often fall short.† Yet, however inadequate our thoughts and words may be we *can* humbly and with thanks speak of God. We can — indeed we should — joyously praise Him for who He is. And the essays in this book, collectively, rightly speak of and praise Him as the God of holy love.

From time to time, both historically and presently, students of the Bible and theologians seek to understand the greatness of God by identifying one attribute which, in a sense, summarizes or encompasses the aggregate whole of the divine attributes.‡ One of the attributes which is often understood in this way is holiness. The seraphim of Isaiah 6:3 call to one another, "Holy, holy, holy is the LORD Almighty; the whole earth is full of his glory." "Day and night" the four living creatures of Revelation 4:8 "never stop saying: "'Holy, holy, holy is the Lord God Almighty,'" who was, and is, and

---

* J. Scott Duvall and J. Daniel Hays, *God's Relational Presence: The Cohesive Center of Biblical Theology* (Grand Rapids, MI: Baker Academic, 2019), 325, emphasis added; also see 1-2, and 4-8. Whether or not one agrees with Duvall and Hays that this is "the" cohesive center of the Bible, they clearly illustrate that God's relational presence is a pervasive and fundamental affirmation of Scripture.

† Respectful of the Otherness of God and of the limitations of human thought and language, apophatic theology or the *via negativa* constitutes a mystical approach to theology, often formulated in statements of negation rather than statements of affirmation. While not isolated to Eastern Orthodox Christianity, apophatic theology is particularly prominent in the Orthodox tradition.

‡ It would not be a bad idea at this point to remind ourselves of the importance of theological humility, one example of which is described in the preceding footnote.

is to come.'" The God of the Scriptures is utterly unique, utterly Other in His holiness. It is not surprising that some of God's people sum up the goodness and glory of God by echoing the heavenly host, proclaiming, "Holy, Holy, Holy is the Lord God Almighty!"

There is a second attribute which is sometimes regarded as being "the attribute of attributes": divine love. In Psalm 136 it seems that the psalmist cannot say it enough. Worshippers are led in every verse — twenty-six times — "His love endures forever." The gospel writer John gives us a glimpse of the nature of the eternal relationship between Jesus and His Father, who is also our Father, by letting us know that Jesus knew that the Father had "loved [Him] before the creation of the world" (John 17:24). Earlier in his gospel account, John himself sets forth an affirmation which has become for many Christians a quintessential summary of the message of salvation: "For God so loved the world that he gave his one and only Son, that whoever believes in him shall not perish but have eternal life" (Jn. 3:16).* It is understandable that some of God's people confidently proclaim, "God is love!"

Without presuming to speak for the editor of this book or the other contributors, it seems not inappropriate to suggest that the leitmotif of the book reflects a view which appreciates both of these lines of thought and praise while also regarding each of them, taken by themselves, as incomplete. Thus, the leitmotif of this book is holy love — the reality of God's holy love and the potential for our holy love. When considering the economies of God one can rightly understand and appreciate His holiness only by being open to the embrace of His Love, and one cannot rightly understand and appreciate His love

---

* Some scholars believe that the quotation rendered by John in verses 10-15 continues through verse 21, and thus that these words of verse 16 were those of Jesus Himself.

without being awe-struck by His holiness. In *The Theology of John Wesley*, Kenneth Collins rightly observes that "the term 'holy love' is not a simple and straightforward expression but involves a conjunction that is expressed in the ideas of separation for the sake of purity and communion for the sake of love."* Just as God is both transcendent and immanent, so too He is both "Other" in His holiness and "not far from any one of us" (Acts 17:27) in His personal presence.

Even if one can largely nod in agreement with the preceding half-dozen paragraphs it would be understandable at this point to be asking, "But what does this have to do with 'The Ivory Tower'?" A fair question, the response to which will seek to address both some of the perspectives and assessments explicitly reflected in descriptions of this "tower" as, for example, "irrelevant" or "impractical" or "cut-off from the real world," as well as some of the more subtle, perhaps never explicitly stated, beliefs behind such perceptions.

As observed above, the God whom we worship is omnipresent, immanent, and relationally present in this world. While few Christians may consciously or overtly deny these realities, a lightly stated but deeply held caricature of "The Ivory Tower" as a place which is cut off from "the real world" may reflect the view — however subtly or implicitly held — that it is a place cut off from the presence and work of God. This kind of subtle, perhaps unconscious failure to believe and trust deeply in God's engaged presence throughout the world is not unique to assessments of academic institutions. There are many Christians who *in theory* affirm the omnipresence of the living God, but who deep inside seriously doubt that God is in fact

---

* Kenneth J. Collins, *The Theology of John Wesley: Holy Love and the Shape of Grace* (Nashville, TN: Abingdon, 2007), 8.

present and at work in Hollywood or Washington, D.C., or public schools or movie theaters or scientific laboratories, or . . . name the realm or arena where God most certainly cannot be because it's "such a bad place." To the contrary, as His Son's incarnation in this world revealed, the God whom we worship is omnipresent and out-reaching in His love, despite the dishonoring of His holiness.

Furthermore, if this God is the God of holy love, it means that holy love is present and at work in the world, including Hollywood and Washington, D.C., and public schools and movie theaters and scientific laboratories. And in the so-called "Ivory Tower." This is not to claim that holy love will always be readily evident. It is not to claim that everyone who studies and works in the academy — including Christians who study and work in the academy — will seek or manifest God's holy love. It is, however, to claim that God is not absent from the arenas of academic and scholarly work and that the "tower" is very much within the reach of God's holy love. Another way to state this is simply to recognize that, theologically speaking, "The Ivory Tower" does not exist. It is a caricature. It is a myth. The good news is that it is a myth which can be replaced by recognizing that the academy is an arena — in no way the only arena, but one arena — into which God can and does reach with His holy love.

The People and Work of the Academy

The first observation to be made in this second part of the essay may seem unnecessary, but it is not. It is this: The students and faculty who carry out academic and scholarly work are human beings. They are people. Just as it has been important to state certain truths about God, so too it is necessary here to explicitly affirm the full and genuine humanity of students and scholars. It is necessary because caricatures of academic institutions as somehow separate from "the real world" often carry with them the caricature, whether stated or not, that people whose primary activities are academic are somehow fundamentally "different" — not quite like the rest of us — or that the conditions and types of work carried out in academic institutions somehow shields or protects people from the harsher realities of life. But this is simply not the case. I have, for example, both read about and personally know many Christian scholars who have suffered the same kinds of trials and afflictions that . . . well, that other people suffer.* There is no tower into which anyone, including scholars and students, can escape to be safe from the harshest realities of life. But, as observed earlier the holy love of God can and does reach into all arenas, including the people and the work of institutions of higher learning.

For our purposes here we will consider academic and scholarly work as consisting largely in two forms of endeavor: seeking knowledge and communicating knowledge. First, some perspective on seeking knowledge. Love that echoes God's love "rejoices in the truth" (1 Corinthians 13:6). Christ-followers should be lovers of the truth. This does not require one to be a professional scholar or a student enrolled in an academic program. But those Christians who are scholars or students should be and usually are motivated by a love of truth, a love of knowledge.

One Christian scholar puts it this way: "Our interest in

---

* There is a sizeable body of literature by scholars recounting their own personal tragedies, and these are only those who make the decision to so write. At my modest-sized institution alone, I have two colleagues who have written such books. Don Payne wrote *Surviving the Unthinkable: Choosing to Live After Someone You Love Chooses to Die* (Eugene, OR: Resource Publications, 2015) about his brother's suicide, and Douglas Groothuis wrote *Walking Through Twilight: A Wife's Illness — A Philosopher's Lament* (Downers Grove, IL: InterVarsity, 2017) about his wife's early-onset dementia and subsequent death.

scholarship lies not simply in exploring a topic academically. It is fueled by a quest for God's truth for the sake of arriving at important insights, clearing up prevailing misconceptions, or both."* This love, as all others, is made possible by and subject to the holy love of God and, when rightly ordered, it is one genuine form of love. In their discussion of the love of knowledge, Robert Roberts and Jay Wood rightly observe that "Christian tradition, starting with the Bible, has commended a discriminating appetite for knowledge."† They illustrate this by highlighting the apostle Paul's list of things about which we are to think, beginning with "whatever is true" (Philippians 4:8). For many scholars and students, a holy love for the truth leads them — indeed, in a holy way it compels them — into study, into reading, into research.

Like all loves, the love of knowledge can be disordered. It can be corrupted. Apart from an acknowledgment of and thanks for the holy love of God, the love of knowledge can lead one to pursue knowledge in a way that neglects other goods or that results in an unholy pride. However, in the words of Andreas Köstenberger, "Because of our pursuit of holiness, there should be a strategic concern not to neglect our personal responsibilities in all the various areas of our lives."‡ As for pride, a holy love of knowledge will be grounded in and conducted with a keen sense of humility. Mindful that the fear of God is the beginning of both knowledge and wisdom, scholars motivated by holy love pursue knowledge with a keen sense of both dependence and limitations.§ Thus, holy love echoed in holy

---

* Andreas J. Köstenberger, *Excellence: The Character of God and the Pursuit of Scholarly Virtue* (Wheaton, IL: Crossway, 2007), 63.

† Robert C. Roberts and W. Jay Wood, *Intellectual Virtues: An Essay in Regulative Epistemology* (Oxford: Oxford University Press, 2007), 155.

‡ Köstenberger, *Excellence*, 64.

§ Experientially, and to a degree that is difficult for people outside the academic arena to

love of the truth propels and guides students and scholars in the pursuit of knowledge. But love does not stop there.

Stephanie Paulsell, of Harvard Divinity School, suggests that "academic work done not for some external reward but out of a desire for a deeper life with God and others, is a pearl of great price, worthy of the sacrifice of our time and resources to pursue."[*] The words to be highlighted here are "and others." Even though academic study and research often requires a great deal of individual work and even though it often provides the scholar with its own pleasures, academic work is not meant to be kept to oneself. Indeed, in most instances scholars are required to share their work, to communicate about their work, with others. The "professional" purposes of this sharing include accountability and improvement. However, when holy love is motivating academic work, the fruit of scholarly work is also shared out of care for others, out of a distinctive kind of generosity.

This is done in a variety of ways, such as teaching, publishing, or participating in organizations whose purpose is to disseminate knowledge to varied publics. When motivated by holy love (and grounded, of course, in rigorous research and careful thought) these activities are neither grandstanding nor a manipulative assertion of power. Rather, as Roberts and Wood observe, "The love of knowledge would not be in the fullest sense an intellectual virtue in a person who loved it only for himself." A scholar impelled by holy love also has "concerns for the cognitive well-being of other people." Thus, "love of knowledge is not just a love of epistemic

---

appreciate, there is also the tendency to be humbled by working in a context where one's work is subject to rigorous assessment and close critique by peers.

[*] Stephanie Paulsell, "Writing as a Spiritual Discipline," in *The Scope of Our Art: The Vocation of the Theological Teacher*, eds. L. Gregory Jones and Stephanie Paulsell (Grand Rapids, MI: Eerdmans, 2002), 23. Paulsell is here drawing upon the reflections of the French thinker and activist Simone Weil.

goods as such, but of other people's having them."* Scholarly work flowing from holy love seeks the good of others.

Conclusion

As noted in the introduction, this essay is both descriptive and aspirational. It is descriptive in that there are many people who fulfill and model the values of scholarly work done out of holy love. It is aspirational in that there is always room for holy love to more fully shape scholars and scholarship and for that scholarship to inform the exercise of holy love both within and beyond the so-called "Ivory Tower."

This essay has been a pleasure to write because the person whom this book honors has been and continues to be shaped and empowered by holy love, and his research, writing, teaching, and preaching have been and continue to be motivated and shaped by holy love. Because of this and because he has always sought, in the power of the Holy Spirit, to serve others, he both exemplifies the descriptive portions of this essay and models a way toward the realization of the aspirational elements of this essay.

Soli deo gloria

W. David Buschart is Professor of Theology and Historical Studies at Denver Seminary. His most recent book, co-authored with Kent D. Eilers, is Theology as Retrieval: Receiving the Past, Renewing the Church *(Downers Grove, IL: InterVarsity Academic, 2015). Both David and his wife Nancy, a spiritual director, are ruling elders of Cherry Creek Presbyterian Church, Greenwood Village, Colorado.*

---

* Roberts and Wood, *Intellectual Virtues*, 164-165.

CHAPTER TEN

Holy Love and Church History: The Curious Case of Edward Irving

Jerome Van Kuiken

Tribute

Bill Ury's reputation preceded him. When I moved to Mississippi to attend seminary, I'd already heard about his brilliance expressed in seven-word-per-second lectures punctuated with top-shelf concepts and vocabulary like "the ubiquity of overarching and underpinning motifs in the un-bifurcated coinherence of isness". In his philosophy course, I studied trinitarian metaphysical and cultural analysis. In his systematic and historical theology courses, I studied trinitarian doctrine and its development. Then I took a course on his dissertation, "Trinity, Personhood and Relationships." By then, I had joined his discipleship group and experienced firsthand how he lived out his faith in persons-in-a-communion-of-holy-love. It was a compelling theological vision and lifestyle that spoiled me for anything less. That semester, my first child had the excellent timing to be born during final exam week. When Bill called the hospital to congratulate us, I explained that I hadn't really missed his exam, I'd just made it practical — with my wife, my baby, and myself, we had a trinity with plenty of personhood and relationships going on! Both his pastoral call to the hospital and the freedom I felt to respond humorously signal the other side of Bill's character: not merely a brilliant mind but a godly, compassionate, and life-loving heart. Besides the hospital call, my favorite memories are of his responding to a loss of lighting by leading a class in singing, "Jesus Wants Me for a Sunbeam" and, the time my wife and I babysat his kids, his getting down on eye level with his three-year-old to give instructions using a child-appropriate vocabulary. Instead of "isness," he spoke of going to "beddy." I get pedagogical mileage out of that latter memory whenever I teach on divine accommodation in revelation. Bill practiced what he preached, even unawares. That's his greatest legacy to us, his grateful students.

Essay
Introduction

Edward Irving (1792-1834) was a Scottish Presbyterian minister in London in the early 1800s. His dramatic preaching style transformed his tiny congregation into a megachurch, but his novel theological views rapidly led to derision by society, division within his congregation, and defrocking by his denomination on charges of heresy.* His advocacy of charismata such as glossolalia, prophecy, and apostleship, available through a post-conversion baptism with the Holy Spirit, anticipated the Pentecostal and Charismatic Movements.† His claim that in the Incarnation, Christ assumed a fallen, even sinful, human nature has been revisited in contemporary mainstream theology due to the massive influence of Karl Barth, who repeated Irving's claim while significantly modifying its meaning.‡ As we shall see, Irving's pneumatology and Christology both relate to his view of Christian sanctification as holy love.

Christ's "Sinful Flesh"

Irving affirms that in the Incarnation, God the Son assumed a human nature exactly the same as ours. But ours is a fallen nature, subject to total depravity and its effects, guilt, suffering, and mortality. Therefore, Christ's humanity, too, was characterized by these defects. In this way His being "in the likeness of sinful flesh" (Romans 8:3), "made sin" (2 Corinthians 5:21), and bearing "our sins in his body"

---

* Biographies of Irving include (Margaret) Oliphant, *The Life of Edward Irving*, 2nd ed., rev. in 2 vols. (London: Hurst and Blackett, 1862); A. L. Drummond, *Edward Irving and His Circle* (n.p.: James Clarke, [1936]); H. C. Whitley, *Blinded Eagle: An Introduction to the Life and Teaching of Edward Irving* (Chicago: Alec R. Allenson, 1955); Arnold Dallimore, *The Life of Edward Irving: Fore-runner of the Charismatic Movement* (Edinburgh: Banner of Truth, 1983); and Tim Grass, *The Lord's Watchman*, Studies in Evangelical History and Thought (Milton Keynes, UK: Paternoster, 2011). Grass's is the best-balanced; the rest tend toward one-sided praise or critique.
† C. Gordon Strachan, *The Pentecostal Theology of Edward Irving* (London: Darton, Longman & Todd, 1973); Dallimore, *Life*; Grass, *The Lord's Watchman*, chs. 16-18.
‡ E. Jerome Van Kuiken, *Christ's Humanity in Current and Ancient Controversy: Fallen or Not?* (London: Bloomsbury T&T Clark, 2017).

(1 Peter 2:24) are *ontologically*, not merely *forensically* true.* The "evil powers inherent in flesh" in its fallen state,† its sinful inclinations, were a perpetual source of temptation to Him until sin was rooted out by the ontological change wrought by the Resurrection.‡ Irving is careful to insist, however, that although Christ's human *nature* was sinful, His *person* remained unstained by sin.§ The ground of this distinction lies in the traditional Christological claim that in the Incarnation, the divine Logos assumed *an hypostatic* humanity — a human nature but not a human person, with the Logos Himself supplying the personhood in the man Christ Jesus.⁵

Christ's Sanctifying Spirit

Not only was the person of the earthly Christ sinless. Prior to His resurrection, His humanity was continuously being made sinless by the sanctifying action of the Holy Spirit. Irving rejects his critics' view that Christ's human nature was sanctified decisively at the moment of conception so that thereafter no sin was present in it. This view, Irving claims, postulates a "physical change" that would destroy Christ's consubstantiality with us, including His liability to being tempted as we fallen sinners are (Hebrews 4:15).** Such a beginning to Christ's earthly life also would render its end redundant: "For if in

---

*   Edward Irving, *Christ's Holiness in Flesh, the Form, Fountain Head, and Assurance to Us of Holiness in Flesh* (Edinburgh: John Lindsay, 1831), xxvi-xxix, 1-2, 37, 45, 55-58. Cf. Edward Irving, *The Collected Works of Edward Irving*, ed. G. Carlyle (London: Alexander Strahan, 1864), 5:146-147, 152, 174, 319-321, 330-331, 335.

†   Irving, *Christ's Holiness in Flesh*, 28.

‡   Irving, *Works*, 5:160-163; Irving, *Christ's Holiness in Flesh*, xxx, 40, 93.

§   Irving, *Christ's Holiness in Flesh*, vii-viii, xi, xxvi.

⁵   Irving, *Works*, 5:3, 115-116.

** Irving, letters to a Mr. Macdonald (May 21, 1830) and to Thomas Chalmers (June 2, 1830), in Oliphant, *Life*, 2:123-124, 138, respectively; Irving, *Christ's Holiness in Flesh*, 37-38, 79-81.

his conception the particles of his flesh were changed from unholy to holy, from mortal to immortal, then what was left to be done at the resurrection?"[*]

Instead, Irving sets forth his own view "that in Christ there was the law of sin and death, which the law of the Spirit of life did ever prevail against . . .; and that the thing spoken of in the holy Scriptures as holiness, is nothing else than the putting down of the law of sin and death in the members, by the law of the Spirit of life in the mind."[†] Elsewhere he describes Christ's experience in a manner anticipatory of a modern sewage treatment plant:

> Christ who, through his flesh, doth receive the gathering streams of all corruption, doth feel their approach, is conscious of their vileness, is terrified and agonised by their number and aggravation, doth feel them as his own, doth cry out on their account, yea doth confess them as his own in the book of Psalms, the only record of his inward man; and yet is not overwhelmed with them, though sorely grieved, but ever as they come hath power to convert them into streams of living waters, which he sendeth forth for the refreshing of all living.[‡]

Consequently, the sinful impulses within Christ's flesh never produced actual sinning by His person.[§]

Crucial to Irving's account of Christ's sanctification is that the

---

[*] Edward Irving, "On the Human Nature of Christ," in *Morning Watch* 1, Mar. 1829, 97.
[†] Irving, *Christ's Holiness in Flesh*, 38-39; cf. 60, 73-74, 78. On 42-43, he specifically rejects any idea of the "eradication" of sin in Christ's flesh during His earthly lifetime; rather, fleshly sin was in a state of enforced "impotency," like a sacrificial animal bound to the altar.
[‡] Irving, *Christ's Holiness in Flesh*, 28.
[§] Irving, *Works*, 5:126-127, 169-173, 245; Irving, *Christ's Holiness in Flesh*, 43; Edward Irving, *The Day of Pentecost, Or, The Baptism with the Holy Ghost* (London: Baldwin & Cradock, 1831), 9.

Spirit alone, not any divine power of the Son's own, is its source. Irving holds a kenotic Christology in which the Logos reduces His abilities to those of a mere human being. The Holy Spirit condescends to submit to the Son of Man *as a man*, not as the divine Son, in a manner prototypical for Christians of their God-given authority to make use of the Spirit for their own sanctification and empowerment,[*] even to the point of possessing "perpetual infallibility of thought, speech, and behaviour"![†]

Implications for Christian Life

Irving saw specific pastoral implications to his theology. If, as his opponents claimed, Christ's human nature were not sinful, then it must be His alien, sinless humanity that is the object of God's salvific affection rather than our own sin-tarnished human nature. But if Christ truly has shared in our postlapsarian lot, then we may trust confidently in His sympathetic mediation, hope in a future resurrection like His, and follow His example now through Spirit-empowered lives of holy love.[‡]

At his church trial for heresy, Irving powerfully illustrated this last point:

> This is no question of scholastic theology. I speak for

---

[*] Irving, *Works*, 2:220; 4:531-538; 5:87-89, 112-113, 124, 132-134, 256, 437-440; Irving, *Christ's Holiness in Flesh*, 39; Irving, *Day of Pentecost*, 16, 28-32, 41, 62, 64, 70, 76, 90. In *Works*, 4:537, Irving retracts any previous statements which may suggest that Christ defeated sin by His divinity rather than by His humanity alone.

[†] Irving, *Day of Pentecost*, 54; cf. 30-32, 42, 53-55, 65; Irving, *Works*, 5:256. In *Day of Pentecost*, 55, Irving explicitly insists that infallibility is not reserved for the Pope but is the common privilege of all Christians.

[‡] Irving, *Works*, 4:526-558; 5:128, 132-133, 438; Irving, *Christ's Holiness in Flesh*, *passim*; Irving, *Day of Pentecost*, *passim*. See Irving, *Works*, 4:541-559 for a moving meditation on Christian life as a sharing in the holy, self-sacrificial love of Christ.

the sanctification of men. I wish my flock to be holy; and, unless the Lord Jesus has contended with sin, as they are commanded to do, how can they be holy when they follow Him? Can I ask the people to do or suffer more than He did? He is the Captain of their salvation, and I wish them to follow Him! Can a soldier who is sick, wounded, or dead, be expected to follow a leader who is filled with the omnipotence of God? Nay! But if his captain be sick, wounded, and dead, too, may he not ask the soldier to do the like? Now Jesus was sick for us, contended with sinful flesh for us, and hence it is that He can call on us to follow Him in our contendings [*sic*] with sin, our sicknesses, and deaths.*

Ironically, a man on trial for impugning Christ's sinlessness was keen on promoting Christians' holiness. Elsewhere he critiques his own Reformed tradition for overemphasizing believers' persisting sinfulness. Rather, he insists that God commands and therefore makes possible that fallen beings live in perfection of holiness in this life, a perfection entered through regeneration and contradicted whenever Christians yield to sin.† Irving sees his Christology as countering both despair and pride over one's spiritual state: we need not despair of being holy despite our sinful flesh, for Christ was holy in the same flesh as ours; and we dare not stand aloof in "Pharisaical pride" at our holiness, for Christ's own holiness did not cause Him to distance Himself from our sinful flesh.‡

---

* Irving's defense at his trial (March 13, 1833), in Oliphant, *Life*, 2:346. Cf. Irving, *Works*, 4:536-539; *Works*, 5:141, 145-146.

† Irving, letter to Marcus Dods (March 8, 1830), in Oliphant, *Life*, 2:114; Irving, *Works*, 1:623-624, 644; Irving, *Christ's Holiness in Flesh*, 6-9, 42, 69-72.

‡ Irving, letter to his sister Elizabeth (March 27, 1833), in Oliphant, *Life*, 2:358.

Irving thinks that the Wesleyan doctrine of sanctification particularly leads to such latter-day Pharisaism:

> For... if you are ashamed to think the holy soul of Jesus should inhabit mortal and corruptible flesh, ... then you will be also ashamed, after you have been sanctified of the Holy Ghost, to confess the sinfulness of your own flesh, but will think and believe, with the Arminians, that it hath received a purification... and, thus purified, you will loathe to mingle again with publicans and sinners, lest you should be tainted anew; and you will say, "Stand off: I am holier than thou."*

In short, Irving detects in the Wesleyan view of the sanctification of Christians the same troubled concept of sanctification as ontological change that bedevils his Christological critics' view of the sanctification of Christ's humanity *in utero*. In both cases, the result is the alienation of those having the resources to save (Christ and His saints) from those having the need to be saved (those burdened by the weight of sin).

A Wesleyan Appraisal

How may Wesleyans respond to Irving? We should commend him first for calling Christians to a presently available holy lifestyle of victory over sin. In this and in his supporting exegesis of such texts as Matthew 5:48 and 1 John 1:7-2:2, Irving hews close to Wesley.†

---

* Irving, *Works*, 5:127. For the lumping together of Arminians and Methodists, see *Works*, 5:77. For Irving's critique of the "abominable notion of the Wesleyan Methodists" regarding conditional security, see *Works*, 5:196.

† Cf. Irving, *Christ's Holiness in Flesh*, 5-8, 69 with John Wesley, *Plain Account of Christian Perfection* in John Wesley, *The Works of John Wesley*, 3rd ed. (London: Wesleyan Methodist Book Room, 1872; repr., Grand Rapids: Baker, 1986), 11:376, 390, 444. Throughout this

The emphasis afforded to the Holy Spirit, the agent of sanctification, is also welcome to those whose tradition has been influenced by the likes of John Fletcher and Phoebe Palmer. Furthermore, Irving calibrates Christian holiness to the earthly life of Jesus, a critical move if one is to avoid framing one's expectations of Christian life according to notions foreign to the faith. Irving's view of Christ-defined holiness as engaging with sinners rather than avoiding them certainly rings true to the New Testament, and his critique of Pharisaical Arminians bears an uncomfortable resemblance to some — though by no means all! — Wesleyan-Holiness practice.*

On the other hand, Irving's own thought veers perilously near Gnosticism with his talk of a post-mortem "physical change" to the very "particles of [Christ's] flesh" being necessary in order to eliminate its sin. Nazarene theologian Mildred Wynkoop has taught Wesleyans to beware of conceptualizing sin as a quasi-material entity to be removed rather than as an affective disposition to be reoriented.† Such a reorientation is compatible with continued existence in a mortal body and fallen world.

Irving is able to affirm a continuous conversion of sinful into sinless desires throughout Christ's and Christians' lives. The underlying sin inherent in human nature, however, can only be suspended, not destroyed, in this life. But if this is so, then Christ's sinlessness is radically relativized, for there remains a fundamental element of His being

---

essay, I cite the most generally accessible rather than the yet-to-be-completed critical edition of Wesley's writings.

* Indeed, The Salvation Army was founded a few decades later in the same city in which Irving had ministered and in opposition to the same exclusionary practice of holiness by English Methodists that he had decried.

† See, e.g., Mildred Bangs Wynkoop, *A Theology of Love: The Dynamic of Wesleyanism* (Kansas City, MO: Beacon Hill, 1972), ch. 8. Even Wynkoop's critic Richard S. Taylor, "Why the Holiness Movement Died," *God's Revivalist*, March 1999 (repr., Cincinnati: Revivalist Press, 1999), 14-15, agrees with the point above.

that passively, if not actively, resists God and incurs divine judgment. Given this point, Irving's attempted distinction between sinfulness of nature and sinlessness of person fails, for according to his reading of the Psalms, Christ "doth feel [corrupt desires] as *his own* . . . doth confess them as *his own*"; that is, He does not excuse them as belonging to His nature rather than His person but takes *personal* responsibility for them. In the end, then, Christ's death is for His own sin and His spotlessness as both priest and sacrifice comes into question.

What would Wesley have thought of Irving's view of Christ's sinful flesh? Although Wesley died the year before Irving's birth, during his lifetime he encountered a similar perspective from his one-time mentor William Law (1686-1761), whose writings later may have influenced Irving's view.* Law penned a pair of books that communicated to his British readers the teachings of the Continental Kabbalist mystic Jakob Boehme. In his books, Law repeatedly describes Christ's incarnation in a manner that anticipates Irving's language. Here is but one example:

> He was made Man for our Salvation, that is, He took upon Him our fallen Nature, to bring it out of its *evil crooked* State. . . . If the Life of fallen Nature, which Christ had taken upon Him, was to be overcome by Him, then every Kind of suffering and dying, that was a giving up, or departing from the Life of fallen Nature, was . . . necessary . . .. And therefore the Sufferings and Death of Christ were, in the Nature of the Thing, the only possible Way of his [*sic*] acting contrary to, and overcoming all the Evil that was in the fallen State of Man.†

---

* Van Kuiken, *Christ's Humanity*, 9-11.

† William Law, *The Spirit of Prayer and The Spirit of Love*, ed. Sidney Spencer (repr.

Aghast at these books' assorted theosophical speculations and heterodox tendencies, Wesley published a rebuttal and warned his Methodists to steer clear of the teachings of Law and Boehme. Yet for whatever reason, he never addressed Law's account of Christ's humanity.[*]

When he does write elsewhere of the Incarnation, Wesley claims that Christ was "made in the likeness of the fallen creatures" in their disgrace, sufferings, temptations, and "innocent infirmities."[†] Despite His likeness to our sinful flesh, however, He was "pure from sin."[‡] In that case there is hope for our own liberation from sin amid the same conditions. Wesley would concur with Irving that an element of sin remains in believers subsequent to their regeneration, but he would disagree with Irving's belief that regeneration effects as much perfection in holiness as is available this side of eternity. The discovery of remaining sin, Wesley taught, should drive one to seek an "entire" sanctification, a "perfect love," a full sharing in the "mind of Christ," in whom no sinful disposition found room.[§] Like Christ, fully sanctified Christians experience temptation and "thoughts concerning evil" while free of "evil thoughts" that express an evil heart.[¶] Like Him, they remain limited in knowledge and

---

Cambridge: James Clarke, 1969), 249 (italics original); cf. 35, 47, 190, 250.

[*] His expansive critique of Law's two books appears in Wesley, *Works* 9:466-518. For analyses of Law's influence on and clashes with Wesley, see J. Brazier Green, *John Wesley and William Law* (London: Epworth, 1945); Eric W. Baker, *A Herald of the Evangelical Revival: A Critical Inquiry into the Relation of William Law to John Wesley and the Beginnings of Methodism* (London: Epworth, 1948).

[†] John Wesley, *Explanatory Notes upon the New Testament* (repr., London: Epworth, 1948), 730 (Phil 2:7), 25 (Matt 4:1), 821 (Heb 4:15), 304 (John 1:14); 821 (quotations from pp. 730 and 821, respectively); cf. 822-823 (Heb 5:7-8); Wesley, *Plain Account* in *Works*, 11:419.

[‡] Wesley, *Explanatory Notes*, 546 (Rom 8:3); cf. 830 (Heb 7:26), 910 (1 John 3:5).

[§] Sermons 13 ("On Sin in Believers") and 14 ("The Repentance of Believers") in Wesley, *Works*, 5:144-70; Wesley, *Plain Account* in *Works*, 11:380-387, 401-3, 423.

[¶] Sermon 40 ("Christian Perfection") in Wesley, *Works* 6:16.

must practice resignation, "the last lesson which our blessed Lord (as man) learnt while He was upon earth. He could go no higher than, 'Not as I will, but as thou wilt.'"* For Wesley, Christlikeness is compatible with human life under fallen conditions.

The primary attraction of Irving's doctrine of Christ's sinful flesh is surely experiential. There is comfort in knowing that Christ has gone through all that we do. Or has He? If, as Irving claims, Christ never actually sinned, then arguably the *majority* of human experience eludes Him. He knows nothing of the initial thrill of temptation yielded to — the sweetness of stolen water (Proverbs 9:17) — and the later misery consequent upon wrongdoing, or the temptations peculiar to those already habituated to a certain sin. The premise that one can only sympathize with and be a role model for persons in conditions that one has personally experienced bears scrutiny, for it leads to the conclusion that Christ must be *exactly* like us in every way, to the extent of actually sinning.† And if He is just the same as us, then can He truly save us or merely empathize?‡ Irving's illustration at his trial points up the problem. How can a dead captain lead dead troops? Would a soldier really wish to follow an invalid into combat?

As we have seen, Irving's solution to Christ's kenotic weakness is the Spirit's power. Here too we find experiential attractiveness, now

---

*   Sermon 69 ("The Imperfection of Human Knowledge") in Wesley, *Works* 6:350.

†   As Marilyn McCord Adams asks, "What if God's soteriological task is to redeem by making even horror-filled human lives meaningful? What if God's principal strategy were to sanctify them by metaphysical identification? Wouldn't Incarnation into a human nature that *not only suffers but perpetrates horrors fill that bill?*" in Marilyn McCord Adams, *What Sort of Human Nature? Medieval Philosophy and the Systematics of Christology*, The Aquinas Lecture 1999 (Milwaukee: Marquette University Press, 1999), 98 (emphasis mine). In response, one may note that natures do not perpetrate horrors; persons do. If then, the divine person of the incarnate Christ perpetrates horrors that require redemption, the implication is that even God stands in need of a redeemer and so is not morally and metaphysically ultimate — in short, is not what the Christian tradition has generally meant by the term "God."

‡   S. W. Sykes, "The Theology of the Humanity of Christ," in S. W. Sykes and J. P. Clayton, ed., *Christ Faith and History* (Cambridge: Cambridge University Press, 1972), 61.

based not on Jesus' likeness to us but on our likeness to Him, for we have received the same Spirit as He did and therefore, under Irving's model, can expect to live *exactly* like Him in every way, inclusive of infallibility.* Yet if Christ saves us primarily as a Spirit-filled human being, then was the Incarnation truly necessary? Could we not have saved ourselves with but the assistance of the Holy Spirit? Our being born sinners is not an insuperable obstacle to this line of argument, since for Irving even Christ's sinlessness was only relative.

While Irving held that Christians may be free from all error but not from all indwelling sin, Wesley believed the opposite. In his *Plain Account of Christian Perfection*, he repeatedly urges that sanctification leads to a perfection of love but not of knowledge or manners. The perfect love that replaces a sinful disposition is compatible with errors of judgment, from which arise unintentional transgressions of God's law. These unintentional transgressions merit God's judgment and so require to be covered by Christ's atoning work.[†]

Wesley's acknowledgement of the limits of earthly perfectibility fits well with James' warning that we all err (James 3:2)[‡] and Paul's confession that we do not know how to pray as we ought, but the Spirit intercedes for us (Romans 8:26-27). It also echoes the bedrock *pro nobis* of the gospel: the Lord does for us what we cannot do for ourselves. We imitate Him *analogously*, not *univocally* (as Irving seems to imply), for He and His work remain radically unique.[§]

This raises an unresolved issue within Wesleyan theology, however:

---

* In *Day of Pentecost*, 76, Irving warns that to claim that Christ relied on his own divinity for power during his earthly life is to render him useless as an example.

† Wesley, *Plain Account* in *Works*, 11:374, 383-384, 394-399, 415-419, 442-443.

‡ Cf. Wesley, *Plain Account* in *Works*, 11:375-376, with 417.

§ Ivor J. Davidson, "'Not My Will but Yours be Done': The Ontological Dynamics of Incarnational Intention," *International Journal of Systematic Theology* 7, no. 2 (2005): 203, puts it succinctly: "It is the same Spirit who empowers Jesus who enables other human beings to confess that Jesus and his saving actions are unique."

what is the relationship of sin to infirmity, and what are the implications not only for Christian perfection but also for *Christ's* perfection? Mark K. Olson has traced how Wesley first identified infirmity with sin, then distanced the two in the interest of proclaiming salvation from all sin as available in this life, then finally re-established the link between infirmity and sin "improperly so called" while still affirming a presently possible entire sanctification.* Missing from Olson's fine article is any discussion of Christ's own human infirmities. If all infirmities are inseparable from sin and require atonement, then by sharing in our infirmities, Christ too is sinful and must atone for Himself, as in Irving's view. Wesley, though, distinguishes between our "innocent infirmities" which Christ shared and "sinful infirmity" which He did not.† Probing this distinction may prove fruitful for future research to resolve the tension that Olson has highlighted.

Conclusion

This essay has considered the relationship of Edward Irving's Christology and pneumatology to his account of sanctification. From a Wesleyan perspective, we have found serious deficiencies in his doctrines. Nevertheless, their retrievals and revisions in contemporary Christianity demand that we continue to engage seriously both his teachings themselves and the genuine pastoral concern undergirding them — the concern that Christians embrace the biblical call to Christlike holy love.‡

---

* Mark K. Olson, "John Wesley's Doctrine of Sin Revisited," *Wesleyan Theological Journal* 47, no. 2 (2012): 53-71.

† Wesley, *Explanatory Notes*, 821 (Heb 4:15 [de-italicized], 5:2). This distinction has a precedent in Reformed theology, e.g., Johannes Wollebius, *Compendium Theologiae Christianae*, ch. XVI.3.iii-iv in John W. Beardslee, ed. and trans., *Reformed Dogmatics*, A Library of Protestant Thought (New York: Oxford University Press, 1965), 90.

‡ For a series of attempts to forge consensus on these points, see Van Kuiken, *Christ's Humanity*; E. Jerome Van Kuiken, "All of Him for All of Us: Christ's Person and Offices in

Jerome Van Kuiken was raised in The Philippines as the son of Free Methodist missionaries. He earned his bachelor's degree at Kentucky Mountain Bible College, a Master of Divinity at Wesley Biblical Seminary, and a PhD in Theology at the University of Manchester (UK). For over twenty years he has worked in Christian higher education, most recently as Dean of the School of Ministry and Christian Thought at Oklahoma Wesleyan University. An ordained minister in The Wesleyan Church, he also has served in local churches and as a Bible study leader at camp meetings. He holds professional memberships in the Evangelical Theological Society, the Wesleyan Theological Society, and the Thomas F. Torrance Theological Fellowship. Among his writings are Methodist Christology: From the Wesleys to the Twenty-first Century *(co-edited with Jason Vickers) and regular contributions to the daily devotional* Light From the Word. *He and his wife have two children.*

John Wesley and T. F. Torrance," *Participatio* 4 (2018): 11-38; Jerome Van Kuiken, "Sinless Savior in Fallen Flesh? Toward Clarifying and Closing the Debate," *Journal of the Evangelical Theological Society* 64, no. 2 (2021): 327-40.

CHAPTER ELEVEN

Holy Love and the Evangelical Movement

Roger J. Green

Tribute

Because I am a lifelong soldier (lay member) of The Salvation Army I have been privileged throughout the years to serve on several boards and commissions with The Salvation Army. One of those boards that I still serve on is a board for The Salvation Army's College for Officer Training in Suffern, New York. I first met Bill as we stood in a hotel lobby awaiting transportation to that college.

Bill was also a member, and as we introduced ourselves and spoke, I learned that he had Asbury College connections and that his roommate at Asbury was a Salvationist. It is impossible to attend Asbury without learning something about The Salvation Army. However, I am fairly certain that in his college days he did not envision himself in a Salvation Army uniform!

As the years went by, I witnessed firsthand his love for the Army, and I remember thinking to myself, "Why isn't this fellow a Salvationist?" In fact, in his Methodist years I actually mentioned that to him. He smiled and may at the time have even been pondering that.

Imagine my amazement and delight when I learned that Bill and Diane were indeed going to join the Army. As the years have gone by Bill and I have crossed paths on several occasions at various Army gatherings, and we are both still on the board where we first met. And Bill being Bill — he is always so gracious and affirming whenever he has heard me give a lecture or preach. We were brothers in Christ upon our first meeting, and now I delight that our brotherhood includes servants together in The Salvation Army.

So, I repeat what I have said to both Bill and Diane — "Welcome to the Army and to our work for God's Kingdom."

Essay
Introduction

The term "evangelical" is a perfectly good one with a rich history, beginning with the New Testament. The word *euangelion* is translated gospel, the good news. Mark 1:14-15 proclaims the beginning of Jesus' ministry in this way: "Now after John was arrested, Jesus came into Galilee, preaching the gospel of God, and saying, 'The time is fulfilled, and the kingdom of God is at hand;

repent and believe in the gospel.'" The gospel, therefore, is the good news from our Lord Himself that God's kingdom is at hand with the coming of the Christ.

The term "evangelical" was carried down into the English language by people like William Tyndale, who in 1533 spoke of the evangelical truth, or Sir Thomas More, who in 1532 wrote about Tyndale as his "evangelical brother." Likewise, Martin Luther wrote about the evangelical Church to distinguish Reformation interests from the Roman Catholic Church.

The Eighteenth Century

This paper concentrates on the use of the terms "evangelical" and "evangelicalism" from the eighteenth century to the present. The paper is necessarily limited in its scope. There are, however, several sources for the reader who wants a more complete picture than what will be presented here.*

During the eighteenth century the Wesleyan revival was identified as an evangelical revival, along with the Pietist movement in Germany and the First Great Awakening in America. That Awakening came about through the preaching of Jonathan Edwards in New England, Theodore Frelinghuysen and Gilbert Tennent in New Jersey, and the itinerant British Anglican, George Whitefield. Those preachers came from various denominational backgrounds

---

* See, for example, the five-volume work entitled *A History of Evangelicalism: People, Movements and Ideas in the English-Speaking World* (Downers Grove, IL: InterVarsity Press, 2003-2013). See also Joel A. Carpenter, *Revive Us Again: The Reawakening of American Fundamentalism* (New York: Oxford University Press, 1997); Christian Smith, *American Evangelicalism: Embattled and Thriving* (Chicago: The University of Chicago Press, 1998); and Stanley J. Grenz, *Renewing the Center: Evangelical Theology in a Post-Theological Era* (Grand Rapids, MI: Baker Academic, 2006).

such as Congregationalism, Dutch Reformed, Presbyterianism, and Anglicanism, demonstrating not only the evangelistic thrust of the First Great Awakening, but the impact that the Awakening had across denominational lines. The holy love of God was manifested. through the preaching as well as the response to such preaching.[*]

However, the attention to the term "holy love" in the Wesleyan tradition is Wesley's emphasis on the holy love of God. That theme dominated his theology. Ken Collins emphasized this with the title of his book — *The Theology of John Wesley: Holy Love and the Shape of Grace.*[†] In setting forth his argument in the introduction, Collins writes that "the best and most accurate summarizing word or phrase, and Wesley's ultimate hermeneutic, is not 'love,' as has sometimes been argued, but 'holy love.' Moreover, just as holiness informs love, so, too, does love inform holiness."[‡]

In his sermon entitled *The Love of God,* Wesley challenges us to understand the nature of Holy Love and the response that love demands:

> Are we afraid of loving Him too much! With too fervent, too entire an affection?
>
> Hath the love of God towards us been restrained? Hath He set any bounds to this ocean? Who is He that hath raised us from the dust? Who breathed into us these living souls? Who upholdest us by the word of His power? Who protects us by His gracious providence? Who redeemed us by the blood of His

---

[*] See, for example, Bruce W. Davidson, "Holy Love in the Theology of Jonathan Edwards" *Journal of the Evangelical Theological Society,* Vol. 59, No. 3 (2016): 571-84.
[†] Kenneth J. Collins, *The Theology of John Wesley: Holy Love and the Shape of Grace* (Nashville, TN: Abingdon Press, 2007).
[‡] Collins, *The Theology of John Wesley,* 8.

Son? Who sanctifies us by the grace of His Spirit? O God, are the creatures of Thy hand, the purchase of Thy Son's blood, disputing whether they may not love Thee too much? . . .Yea, worthy art Thou, O Lord, of all the love of all the creatures whom Thou hast made! Especially of those whom Thou hast redeemed! Whom Thou now guidest by Thy counsel, and wilt hereafter receive into Thy glory!*

Collins then goes on to elucidate this central theme of holy love beginning with the God of holy love, moving through creation, the Trinity, humanity's response, and ending with the triumph of holy love in eschatology and glorification. This biblical and Wesleyan emphasis on holy love is not only important as we reflect on the history of the Church but will be crucial as we look forward at what has become of evangelicalism in the twenty-first century.

However, we first need a reminder that the evangelical tradition continued into the nineteenth century with the Second Great Awakening, with both its northern and its southern manifestations. That was followed well into the nineteenth century with the great Finneyite Revival and the revival under the leadership of Dwight L. Moody.

There were some characteristics that manifested themselves throughout these evangelical movements. Four are representative of what is central to evangelical movements, and thereby to the gospel. The first is biblical authority, which takes precedence over the authority of the Church or the authority of any individual. The second is an emphasis on the atonement — God's provision to

---

* John Wesley, "The Love of God" in Albert C. Outer, ed., *The Works of John Wesley*, vols. 1-4, *Sermons* (Nashville, TN: Abingdon Press, 1984-87) 4:339.

bring fallen humanity back to Himself through the life, ministry, suffering, death, resurrection, and ascension of the Word made flesh, even Jesus Christ our Lord. The third is the emphasis on regeneration, the new birth, which is the story of God's free grace available for all humanity. And the fourth is the impulse to share the gospel with our neighbors, both in word and in deed. Holy love insists on returning God's love by loving God and loving our neighbor, and therefore seeking the salvation of our neighbor and justice for all of God's creation.

The Twentieth Century and the Rise of Fundamentalism

A challenge to traditional evangelicalism came at the end of the nineteenth century and the beginning of the twentieth century in England and America. This movement, rooted in British and American Millenarianism, arose out of a fear that the Church had neglected fundamentals of the faith on the one hand, and that the broader culture was becoming more and more godless on the other hand. The battle against both liberal Protestantism and cultural modernism heated up in the twentieth century.

It is clear that some of the leaders of what became known as "fundamentalism," such as Dwight L. Moody and Adoniram Judson Gordon, were men of integrity who bore witness to the glorious Kingdom of God. However, that was not always true as the movement coalesced around some fundamentalist leaders by the time the term fundamentalism became a household name with the publication between 1910 and 1915 of *The Fundamentals*, a ten-volume series of pamphlets, identifying what the authors considered to be the central biblical and doctrinal fundamentals of the Christian faith. As Ernest R. Sandeen wrote, "The defense of Christian doctrine dominated *The Fundamentals,* and the defense of the Bible surpassed any other doctrinal issue."[*]

Protestant fundamentalism was supported by local churches, the founding of Bible Institutes and Colleges, the use of media such as radio programs and the publication of pamphlets and tracts, and the voices of prominent preachers. The Scopes Trial in Dayton, Tennessee in 1925 received national attention and highlighted fundamentalism's war against theories of evolution. Protestantism became sharply divided.

However, as fundamentalism increased in strength and influence, it failed in so many ways. What Sandeen writes of Millenarian leadership could be said of broader fundamentalist leadership into the middle of the twentieth century and beyond. It "did not show the strength of character, deep grasp of and reverence for biblical truth, or intellectual acuity demonstrated by the late nineteenth-century leaders."[†] Such criticism would alone be a challenge to the survival of fundamentalism. But added to that evolved an inability or an unwillingness to be self-critical, an odd view of Scripture often built around the minutiae of prophecy, a preaching of a truncated and pernicious gospel of health and wealth, a lack of sense of the grand history of Christianity, a movement often built around superstars and thereby developing into a cult of personality (many such as Jimmy Swaggart and Jim and Tammy Bakker who would fall into public disgrace), a message often condemning the entire Church, a lack of social responsibility, and a lack of engagement with modern intellectual trends.

---

[*] Ernest R. Sandeen, *The Roots of Fundamentalism: British and American Millenarianism 1800-1930* (Chicago, IL: The University of Chicago Press, 1970), 203.
[†] Sandeen, *The Roots of Fundamentalism,* 269.

Edward J. Carnell, a leader in the movement that broke from fundamentalism, in his book entitled *The Case for Orthodox Theology* "would show that fundamentalism was an aberrant subtype of orthodoxy. He thus defined fundamentalism as 'orthodoxy gone cultic.' It was characterized by 'ideological thinking,' which 'is rigid, intolerant, and doctrinaire.'"*

It could be said that the dangers of this brand of Christianity could have been avoided by one cure — holy love. The biblical message of a loving God who expects love in return for Him and for our neighbors could have permeated the movement of a people who claimed to be contenders for the biblical message. But fundamentalists found themselves at war not only with a fallen culture, but with other Christians, and ultimately among themselves. The battles between Jerry Falwell and Jim and Tammy Bakker in the 1980s became a public controversy on the American scene, and even the most non-religious viewers expected more of love and less of hatred among these preachers of Christian love.

---

* George M. Marsden, *Reforming Fundamentalism: Fuller Seminary and the New Evangelicalism* (Grand Rapids, MI: William B. Eerdmans Publishing Company, 1987), 188-189. A personal encounter with an ultra-fundamentalist came in a flight in Canada several years ago. The gentleman sitting next to me struck up a conversation, and I soon learned from him that the church to which he belonged was the only true church in the world and that God had laid upon him the burden of correcting all other so-called Christians. Following the flight, he sent me a copy of a packet of letters written to several Christian leaders. In his lengthy letter to Billy Graham he wrote "Yes, Mr. Graham, you yourself are a servant of sin (Satan) and serve those that by nature are no Gods and use the name of Christ in vain. . . .. Satan has transformed you into an apostle of Christ while in truth you serve the ruling spirit of this universe." I did not respond!

The Rise of the New Evangelicalism

There arose out of fundamentalism a new movement, holding many of the fundamental biblical doctrines, but determined that the damaged ethos of fundamentalism would be shed and an ethos of holy love would be preached and demonstrated. This movement would eventually name itself "new evangelicalism" and would claim inheritance not only because it held to central biblical doctrines, but because it wanted to reflect the life of the Church since the New Testament, and especially the life of classic historic Protestantism. Rather than retreating from the world, the new evangelicalism aimed at engaging the modern culture with the Good News. The new evangelicals simply could no longer identify themselves as fundamentalists.

There were several leaders of the movement out of fundamentalism. Two notable leaders were Harold J. Ockenga, and Billy Graham, the latter becoming a household name. Although maligned in the most vicious ways by some fundamentalist leaders, these men kept focused on the biblical way forward and attempted in every way possible to concentrate on holy love as they responded to their detractors.

The movement was supported by the founding of the National Association of Evangelicals, Fuller Theological Seminary and *Christianity Today*. Various churches and denominations and colleges, such as Barrington College and Gordon College, as well as seminaries identified themselves as evangelical. The revivalism of Billy Graham reached around the world, and Billy Graham did not react in kind to his fundamentalist critics but stayed the course of preaching the gospel and attempting to love God and neighbor as God gave him the strength to do so. Internationally recognized scholars such as Alister McGrath of Oxford University were known as evangelicals, and McGrath's *Evangelicalism and the Future of Christianity* placed the movement at the center of the history of the Church for the future.

The movement was not without criticism, but that criticism often came from within evangelicalism in attempts to strengthen the movement. Mark Noll's criticism of an intellectual shallowness in the movement in *The Scandal of the Evangelical Mind;* or Donald Dayton's criticism for the failure of evangelicalism to remain faithful to the nineteenth-century social commitments of evangelicalism in *Discovering An Evangelical Heritage;* or David Wells' criticism of evangelicalism's accommodation to the culture in *God in the Wasteland: The Reality of Truth in a World of Fading Dreams* are examples of evangelical writers wanting more from the movement.*

Confusion Sets In

Evangelicalism became part of the story of the wider American culture, and, because of a growing intellectual life began to influence broader Protestantism. However, the public outside of evangelicalism became confused, and with good reason. Fundamentalist leaders had the sense by the end of the twentieth century that the term fundamentalism was not serving them well. The easy solution was to start calling themselves evangelicals. The media was already confused about the meaning of the term (witness such confusion when Jimmy Carter referred to himself as an evangelical), but now the media failed to distinguish in any way between fundamentalism and evangelicalism.

---

* See also Richard J. Mouw's helpful analysis of evangelicalism and fundamentalism in *The Smell of the Sawdust: What Evangelicals Can Learn from Their Fundamentalist Heritage* (Grand Rapids, MI: Zondervan Publishing House, 2000).

Confusion continued for at least two reasons. Many of those fundamentalists who now called themselves evangelicals did not know the history of the term, did not embrace the ethos of new evangelicalism, and continued to exhibit a kind of holy wrath rather than holy love toward their fellow Christians, and sometimes especially toward the new evangelicals.

Second, many of them aligned with the political right, and an undiscerning media simply reported that political allegiance as coming from evangelicals, without regard for the nuance of the term. To the press there was no distinction within evangelicalism between the new evangelicals, who wanted to embrace the characteristics that have been mentioned in this paper, and the fundamentalists, many of whom were exhibiting in even greater measure the criticism of "orthodoxy gone cultic." And for many of those fundamentalists the label evangelical was politicized and contributed to a cultic atmosphere of hatred, antagonism, abuse, and divisiveness, all of which is the opposite of the biblical life in God and His believers of holy love. Such divisiveness brought harm to both the broader Body of Christ and the common good.

New evangelicals were appalled that the term evangelical, with such a genuine biblical meaning and a rich heritage, would be so hijacked and cause such confusion. Therefore, the question arose among those who considered themselves to be evangelicals in the historic meaning of the term, and institutions that had hitherto proudly identified themselves as evangelical, whether the label had now been so corrupted that they no longer wanted to embrace the term for themselves or their institutions.

The Way Forward

Evangelicals have considered dropping the term and identifying themselves by other names, all of which have problems. The name Christian can be a nebulous term without the strength of how the term is used in the New Testament; the label orthodox is a useful term, but in many peoples' minds is related to the Orthodox Church; the term catholic can be helpful, but, like orthodoxy, will be associated with the Roman Catholic Church.

Some evangelicals try to identify what they mean by the term and in that spirit use words like conservative evangelicals, post conservative evangelicals, which means that they are less rigid and more inclusive of other Christians, or open evangelicals, which means that while they embrace biblical authority, and also find grounding in the creeds of the Church and other traditional doctrinal teachings, they are open to broader cultural trends.

There are also many evangelicals who have left the label behind and who have embraced Eastern Orthodoxy or Roman Catholicism. When asked about their pilgrimage they often cite two reasons: they want to be part of the rich two-thousand-year history and tradition of the Church, and they want and need the richer and deeper worship experience than what they found in Protestant evangelicalism.*

I suggest the way forward is twofold: first retain the identity marker evangelical. The term is a rich one going back to the New Testament and represents a powerful Protestant tradition. The Salvation Army, which is my spiritual home, uses the term in its

---

* See Thomas Howard, *Evangelical is Not Enough: Worship of God in Liturgy and Sacrament* (San Francisco, CA: Ignatius Press, 1984). Tom Howard was reared in evangelicalism and became Roman Catholic in 1985 while teaching at Gordon College, an evangelical institution.

international mission statement. The first line states: "The Salvation Army, an international movement, is an evangelical part of the universal Christian Church."* Retaining our identity as evangelical is, I believe, essential even though we constantly have to define the term.

Second, embrace as evangelicals the holy love that is the life of the Church. The second part of The Salvation Army's mission statement reads: "Its message is based on the Bible. Its ministry is motivated by the love of God. Its mission is to preach the gospel of Jesus Christ and to meet human needs in his name without discrimination."† The love of God — that holy love — is at the center of this mission statement. Likewise, as with the term evangelical, we have to keep reminding even our fellow Christians that The Salvation Army is a Christian Church *and* a registered charity. To drop the name simply because people do not understand who we are is unthinkable.

The Salvation Army shares with many other Christians a Wesleyan heritage of costly love. In these troubled times, we embrace the challenge to demonstrate holy love in every way possible. Wesley preached so often on the command to love God and love our neighbor. Kenneth Collins writes, "Consequently, in receiving the holy love of God, as exemplified in justification and the new birth, the chains are broken, the shackles are cracked open, and the soul is set at liberty to love in a godly, empowered way. Wesley holds all of these elements together in the name of love."‡ We in the Wesleyan tradition believe with Wesley that "*love* sits upon the throne. . .and reigns without a rival." With that truth in

---

* *The Salvation Army Handbook of Doctrine* (London, England: Salvation Books) 266.
† *The Salvation Army Handbook of Doctrine,* 266.
‡ Collins, *The Theology of John Wesley,* 227.

mind, Wesley later writes in that sermon,

And, first, if zeal, true Christian zeal, be nothing but the flame of love, then *hatred,* in every kind and degree, then every form of *bitterness* toward them that oppose us, is so far from deserving the name of zeal that it is directly opposite to it. If zeal be only fervent love, then it stands at the utmost distance from *prejudice,* jealousy, evil surmising; seeing 'love thinketh no evil'. Then *bigotry* of every sort, and above all the spirit of *persecution,* are totally inconsistent with it. Let not, therefore, any of these unholy tempers screen themselves under that sacred name. As all these are the works of the devil, let them appear in their own shape, and no longer under the specious disguise deceive the unwary children of God.[*]

Here is holy love manifesting itself in God's love for us and our love for Him in return and for our neighbor. And so, in these turbulent and troublesome times the way of life for any who call themselves evangelical is holy love — love toward those with different political ideas, love toward those who would dismantle government structures, love for those who bear the name of Christian but are so hateful, and love for those who ruthlessly oppose the Christian Church. We say with the hymn writer, George Matheson:

> O Love that wilt not let me go,
> I rest my weary soul in Thee;
> I give Thee back the life I owe,
> That in Thine ocean depths its flow
> May richer, fuller be.[†]

---

[*]   Wesley, *On Zeal* in Outler, ed. *The Works of John Wesley* 3:315-316.
[†]   George Matheson, Song #616 *The Song Book of The Salvation Army* (London: The Salvation Army, 2016).

Roger J. Green is Professor Emeritus of Biblical and Theological Studies at Gordon College in Wenham, Massachusetts. He taught for 46 years, three years at Asbury College and 43 at both Barrington College and Gordon College. While at Gordon College he held the Terrelle B. Crum Chair of Humanities and served for 26 years as the department chair. Dr. Green received his B.A. from Temple University in Philadelphia; his M.Div. from Asbury Theological Seminary; his M.Th. from Princeton Theological Seminary; and his Ph.D. from Boston College. He was awarded the D.D. (honorary) from William and Catherine Booth College (now Booth University College). He is a lifelong member of The Salvation Army, speaks internationally for The Salvation Army, and much of his scholarship has been devoted to the history and theology of The Salvation Army. The Salvation Army recognized him with the Order of the Founder in 2012.

CHAPTER TWELVE

Holy Love and the Salvation Army

Thomas Louden

Tribute

Abundant life is the clear and unmistakable characteristic that I have observed in Bill Ury from the first moment I met him. That moment was in the Fall of 1987 at Asbury College where Bill was the Resident Director for Johnson Dormitories, and I was a resident sophomore in the Johnson Main dormitory. Bill demonstrated an inner fortitude and focus that came through in all he did and spoke. In fact, it was that integrated life of Bill that poignantly spoke and vividly presented the holy love of God. It was through holy love that Bill tenderly confronted me with truth and held me accountable for my living. Bill helped open my eyes to see the beauty of God's holiness and receive His full salvation.

Bill has been continually consistent in living God's abundant life. This consistency has not been more exposed and apparent than within holy matrimony to his beautiful bride, Diane. Bill has modeled for me what it means to be a godly husband living the Pauline doctrine of marriage found in Ephesians 5:21- 33.

Lastly, but perhaps most importantly, Bill has modeled for me what it means to "Be diligent to present yourself approved to God as a worker who does not need to be ashamed, accurately handling the word of truth" (2 Timothy 2:15 NASB). This godly characteristic could possibly be the most profound evidence of the power of the indwelling Christ in Bill's life. The impact of Bill's holy living has shaped my thinking, my understanding, and my pursuit of holy love in my daily living. God has demonstrated through Bill's life that holy love is the key to being a real person, free from intentional sin and living triumphantly until Jesus comes. Thank you, Bill.

Essay

One of the great, if not greatest, privileges of a Salvationist is to be present as one of our Heavenly Father's children receives His Son, Jesus, and is returned to Him. Every man and woman who has been enlisted in this Great Salvation Warfare under the Blood and Fire banner has found within his, or her, heart a passion for the souls of those who live in open and shameless rebellion against God. It is a passion to seek out the lost, the least, and the last with not only great intention, but with orthodox theology and militaristic style strategy, employing the ultimate and effective weapons of love and service.

William Booth, Founder and first General of The Salvation Army, in his vision entitled, *A Vision for the Lost*, articulated his great passion for the lost by proclaiming his life's call to launch into the deep "surging sea of (human sinfulness) ...dark and dangerous. There is no doubt that the leap for you, as for everyone who takes it, means difficulty and scorn and suffering. For you it may mean more than this. It may mean death."* Booth's vision reflected his and his followers' beliefs that God's holy love was the only power to defeat sin, break its hold on humanity, and provide a believer's triumphant living until Christ returns.

In his religious training as a Wesleyan, Booth sought to understand John Wesley's theology of God's grace and unconditional love. He found great solidarity and contentment with Wesley's theology but desired something more of fire and intensity. Booth sensed a lack in the practice of Wesley's theology and sought to apply its maxims to all of humanity, not just those well couched within the church.

Not long after having matured in his faith, Booth began to feel a fire igniting within his heart to proclaim the truth of God and His Holy Love in the open air to the least, the lost, and the last. He declared that "God shall have all there is of William Booth."†

In his seminal work, *In Darkest England and the Way Out*, Booth said,

---

* . William Booth, *Visions* (London: The Salvation Army Book Department, 1906), 159.
† . Roger Green, *The Life and Ministry of William Booth: Founder of The Salvation Army* (United Kingdom: Abingdon Press, 2005), 233.

Holy Love

All the way through my career I have keenly felt the remedial measures usually enumerated in Christian programmes, and ordinarily employed by Christian philanthropy, to be lamentably inadequate for any effectual dealing with the despairing miseries of the outcast classes. The rescued are appallingly few, a ghastly minority compared with the multitudes who struggle and sink in the open-mouthed abyss. Alike, therefore, my humanity and my Christianity, if I may speak of them as in any way separate from each other, have cried out for some comprehensive method of reaching and saving the perishing crowds.[*]

Booth found that the only proper wedding of his orthodoxy and orthopraxy was through complete self-denial, totally embracing the least, lost, and last of society, and preaching an orthodox message of holiness that meant being saved to the uttermost. William took his calling home to his wife, Catherine, and proclaimed to her, "O Kate, I have found my destiny! I offered myself and you and the children up to this great work. Those people shall be our people, and they shall have our God for their God."[†]

From that point forward, holy love and The Salvation Army became united in mission and ministry in the power of the Holy Spirit. This sacred union has called forth men and women to live a servant's life of self-sacrificing love intent on offering to everyone the gift of full salvation through the indwelling presence of the Holy Spirit. Booth envisioned an Army of sanctified hearts of holy love,

---

[*] . William Booth, *In Darkest England and the Way Out* (London: International Headquarters of The Salvation Army, 1890), 2.

[†] . G.S. Railton, *The Authoratative Life of General William Booth* (London: George H. Doran Company, 1912), 56.

which is the key to being a real person as God has intended from creation.

Dr. Dennis Kinlaw, in his book, *This Day with the Master*, said that "Holy Love is the key to being a real person — a complete person. A real person is one who is free from intentional sin."* This powerful transformational holy love of God was the light that awakened William Booth and set him on a lifetime of pursuing the lost to save them and return them to their Heavenly Father.

Holy love and The Salvation Army in the life of William Booth reached around the world and drew the attention of most of the civilized world. The Army grew in exponential ways and became a known entity by many of the most prominent world leaders. Booth, who began his adult life as a pawnbroker's apprentice, became the leader of an unparalleled worldwide movement of God's holy love.

What quality of life could possibly move people around the world to advance the Kingdom in the darkest haunts? How could a life of obscurity and insignificance receive the affection and admiration from the highest offices in the world to the nethermost of human existence? How could an Army, whose greatest weapon was love and service, subdue some of the most powerful strongholds of sin, sickness, poverty, and despair? It is only because of the holy love of God

It was and is God's holy love that draws all people to the Savior who can cleanse them from all sin and fill everyone with His precious Holy Spirit. It was and is God's Holy Love that empowers every believer to live triumphantly and receive abundant life; to live fully human lives without sin. Holy love and The Salvation Army seek to offer to every

---

* . Dennis F. Kinlaw, *This Day with the Master: 365 Daily Meditations* (Grand Rapids: Zondervan, 2002), November 29.

person the key to the incarnation of God in humanity: God wedding Himself to our humanity through His Son, Jesus Christ.

God uniting Himself with humanity is the foundational truth upon which The Salvation Army is founded. General Bramwell Booth said, "… the spirit of The (Salvation) Army — that union of holy love and fiery zeal and practical common sense which, by the power of Christ, provides, wherever it is found, the fruits of Salvation in the bodies and souls of those who are without."*

This holy love spirit found in The Salvation Army is self-evident because it is something that cannot exist without it being proven. Holy love is not only theoretical, but mostly tangible. It is something that is experienced by him who receives it, and it is visible to most, if not all, observers. Holy love, in its essence, is extravagant. Holy love is intended to wed humanity to God and is something that is felt. Everyone who receives God's holy love can give a testimony to its tangible resident reality in their body, mind, and spirit.

These unique and powerful characteristics of holy love are the marks of Christ that can and should be identified with The Salvation Army. Because of holy love, when a person meets a Salvationist, that person should identify holy love because of the Salvationist. And, when a person comes to know holy love, he should identify Salvationists because of holy love. Holy love should be a Salvationists' identity and a Salvationist should be holy love's identity.

General Paul Rader, the fifteenth General of The Salvation Army, expressed the critical need for Salvationists to be identified by holy love and for holy love to be identified by Salvationists.

For what else will distinguish people from all other

---

* . Minnie Lindsay Carpenter, *Kate Lee: The Angel Adjutant of Broken Earthenware* (London: Salvationist Publishing and Supplies, 1950), iv.

people? We're in The Salvation Army wearing our uniforms with pride for we feel that they are a witness; surely, they (our uniforms) say to people 'we're available to you, we're here for you not for ourselves, we're here for you.' That's why we make ourselves known; that's why we identify ourselves so we can be of service. But… the uniform is not enough! If that's the only thing that marks us as the people of God, it's not enough. We need to bear witness by the quality of our lives, by the vitality of our faith, by the experience of the presence of the Spirit of God that God is with us! And, if the glory is gone, all the public kudos and congratulations and contributions and number one ratings in the *Chronicle of Philanthropy* will mean nothing!*

It is with a holy pride that Salvationists wear the uniform, for it speaks to the world of something that is different, someone who is different.

Holy love and The Salvation Army can and must be allies in the Great Salvation War. In every respect, a Salvationist has the greatest opportunities in all the world to bring together God's holy love and the abject desperation of a world separated from God's holy love. It is not, nor can it ever be, a casual or relaxed approach to the redemption of mankind. Holy love and The Salvation Army are meant to be together. The effectiveness and force of this union is unlike anything the world has ever seen, save that of the Lord's own Apostles.

General Evangeline Booth, the seventh of William and Catherine's eight children, expressed the power of holy love and The Salvation Army in the April 1920 issue of *National Geographic*.

---

* . General Paul Rader, *Wearing Our Baptism* (sermon, New York City, June 16, 1996).

Evangeline was asked by the magazine to update the world on the progress of The Salvation Army, and she began by defining the resulted nature of holy love and The Salvation Army.

> For more than half a century the historic banner of The Salvation Army has been raised over the battered towers and broken gates of despairing, wounded humanity, but half of the world never knew about it. It took the blood and agony of a great war (WWI) to demonstrate the fire of a faith which has planted its standard in every country on the earth... (executing) our strategy against insidious foes — poverty, sin, sickness, and despair. It was for that we were called an Army.[*]

Today, the world is no different than that expressed by Evangeline in the words above. We are in desperate need for our Savior and His holy love. The despair, the wars, the rage, the wounds, the need, and growing uncertainties all cry for healing and restoration that holy love and The Salvation Army can offer.

On a warm Sunday evening in Fort Myers, Florida, following the Salvation Meeting, Majors Tom and Julie Anne Louden took their men in the corps alcohol and drug rehabilitation program, *Crossroads*, out for pizza. Major Julie Anne, as she often enjoyed doing, was the bus driver that evening and had just returned to the Red Shield Lodge (RSL) when she quickly observed that something out of the ordinary had taken place and an ambulance was parked at the front entrance. Once she had parked the bus she quickly made her way into the RSL

---

[*] . Evangeline Booth, "Around The World With The Salvation Army," *National Geographic Magazine*, April 1920, 347-68.

and inquired with our security team about the ambulance and asked why it was there. The security officer briefed the major on a very tragic and disturbing event that involved a young woman who had come to the Army in her most desperate time, in need of help.

Major Julie Anne was informed that the young lady who had come into the RSL was clearly traumatized to the point where she was unable to speak and barely able to walk and maintain consciousness. The RSL intake technician attempted to triage this dear lady, but she still could not speak. So, the intake technician wrote on a legal pad, "Do you need help?" The intake technician handed the pad to the young lady and she in response wrote, "Yes!" So, the intake technician immediately called 911 and requested paramedics. The ambulance had just arrived a few moments before the major, and the paramedics were assessing the young lady and preparing her for transport to the hospital.

Major Julie Anne was able to acquire the young lady's name and decided to stop by the hospital later that evening. Major Julie Anne felt an overwhelming urge to go to this precious young woman and offer Jesus to her. After parking the bus at the hospital, Major Julie Anne made her way into the reception area to ask about seeing this young lady and was informed that the hospital had admitted her and invoked the Florida Mental Health Act of 1971, commonly known as the "Baker Act." Major Julie Anne was informed that the Baker Act restricts any non-essential medical personnel from visiting the patient. However, the security guard said, "I see that by your uniform you are a Salvation Army officer. You are one of the most trusted people in our community, so I will let you go back to see her."

When Major Julie Anne arrived at the young lady's room and proceeded in, she observed a most despairing and lifeless person. She immediately made her way to the young lady's bedside, held her hand and said to her, "I don't know what you have been through, but God does, and He loves you and so do I and I am here to help you." Immediately the woman began to weep. She found her voice and the strength to tell her story of abuse, great agony, and despair. As this precious young woman begin to share her story, Major Julie Anne wrapped her arms around her and embraced her with God's love. They both cried. The story that poured out of this precious soul was one of broken trust, abuse, and horrific physical and sexual violations against her. She told of her life with a man whom she loved, and thought he loved her, but instead he abused her regularly and frequently. So, it was on that day she decided it was time for her to escape. She fled from her house on a bicycle without any plan, just ready to run away to somewhere, anywhere. However, tragedy chased her and not long after leaving her home she was followed by a gang of four men who attacked her, abducting her into a wooded area nearby where they raped her repeatedly. It was after that she somehow made it to The Salvation Army's Red Shield Lodge for help.

In reflection, Major Julie Anne testifies that as she felt in her heart the urgency to go to this young woman and offer her Jesus' holy love, she also sensed God's holy love filling her and bringing health, healing, and wholeness again to her own life. She recounts that as she embraced that precious, broken, battered, and beaten soul, and shared God's holy love with her, she also felt His arms embrace her and whisper into her heart, "I see you and I see her and I love you both. I will wipe away every tear." Major Julie Anne says, "That was God's embrace and that was the perfect help that was needed. It was His holy love"*

---

* . Major Julie Anne Louden in discussion with the author, July 2016.

Every Salvationist who is filled to overflowing with God's holy love has the salvation of others in his or her heart. In *The Salvation Army International Annual Report of 1894*, Bramwell Booth, Chief of the Staff, declared "Others" as the watchword for 1895. This annual report was sent to every command in the world and the watchword declaration of "Others" resonated deeply in the hearts of many Salvationists. Holy love is always others-oriented no matter the circumstance. Holy love and The Salvation Army provide the world with Salvationist soldiers who are ready, willing, and able to live out the Army's high ideal of "… holy love, the glorious harvest."[*]

Holy love and The Salvation Army establishes that "the quest for all Salvationists (is) to follow Christ. This is interpreted as seeking the souls of the lost."[†] The quest of Salvationists for lost souls changes the way we see others, the way we listen to others, and what we say and do to others. Holy love and The Salvation Army provides Salvationists the high privilege of displaying self-giving love. "When we find our joy and fulfillment in our relationship with God, then we gain a new freedom to make choices that will open doors of grace for other people. As we make consistent choices based on self-giving love, then the evil diminishes and begins to lose its iron grip on those in our circle."[‡]

Salvationists share a deep joy and fulfillment that is totally and completely predicated upon holy love and The Salvation Army. As was in the heart and life of William and Catherine Booth, so it is

---

[*] . Bramwell Booth, *Papers on Life and Religion* (London: Salvationist Publishing and Supplies, 1920), 1.

[†] . Robert David Rightmire, "Pneumatological Foundations for Salvation Army Nonsacramental Theology," e-Publications@Marquette, Marquette University, published in 1987, accessed February 22, 2022, https://epublications.marquette.edu/dissertations/AAI8716873/.

[‡] . Kinlaw, *This Day with the Master*, November 17.

within the heart and life of every Salvationist who receives the gift of the Holy Spirit and seeks to bring the message of salvation to everyone. William made his last public appearance at Royal Albert Hall in London on May 9, 1912. The 83-year-old Founder of The Salvation Army, in front of a crowd of 7,000, gave his farewell sermon closing with these words that summarized his journey with Holy Love and The Salvation Army:

> While women weep as they do now,
>> I'll fight;
> while little children go hungry as they do now,
>> I'll fight;
> while men go to prison, in and out, in and out, as they do now,
>> I'll fight;
> while there is a drunkard left, while there is a poor lost girl
> on the streets, while there remains one dark soul without the
> light of God,
>> I'll fight — I'll fight to the very end.[*]

William found that a life of holy love in The Salvation Army produced a fighting holiness, a suffering holiness, a soul-saving holiness; in short, Jesus Christ's holiness.[†] Booth's son, Bramwell, expressed the outcome of holy love and The Salvation Army as a person who "…joins together not only to suffer with our Savior on account of the people's sin, but to fight by His side for their redemption."[‡]

---

[*] . The Salvation Army of Texas Divisional Headquarters. "William Booth Makes His Last Public Appearance: On This Day in History, May 9." The Salvation Army. Published on May 9, 2013, accessed on February 22, 2022, https://www.salvationarmytexas.org/blog/william-booth-makes-his-last-public-appearance-on-this-day-in-history-may-9/.

[†] . Rightmire, "Pneumatological Foundations for Salvation Army Nonsacramental Theology."

[‡] . Ibid.

Come now, all people of faith in Jesus Christ, and receive the indwelling presence of the Holy Spirit, receive the holy love of God and endeavor with The Salvation Army to win the world for God.

Major Thomas C. Louden is a lifelong Salvationist and has been an officer in The Salvation Army since 1994. He and his beautiful bride, Major Julie Anne Louden, were united in holy matrimony in 1989 and they are the proud parents of four amazing children, and Marmie and Duke, two astounding grandchildren. Major Louden is an alumnus of Asbury College, Arrow Leadership, The Salvation Army Evangeline Booth College, and The Salvation Army International College for Officers. Major Louden has served as a corps officer, training staff officer, area commander, and general secretary and divisional commander. Currently, Major Louden serves as the President of Evangeline Booth College and Principal for the School for Officer Training. The Loudens most sacred covenants are their marriage, parenting of their children and grandchildren, and officership. They are passionate about the transforming love and power of Jesus Christ and claim Him as their Savior and friend.

CHAPTER THIRTEEN

Holy Love and God's Mission Heart

Robert Lang'at

Tribute

I first met Bill and Diane Ury during a revival meeting at Asbury University during the Fall of 1992. At a tender age, I knew I had met someone who had a deep heart for God and for the nations. It was through his encouragement that I returned five years later to the United States in 1997, to pursue studies at Wesley Biblical Seminary where he served as professor.

Bill exemplified to me the depths of divine love. My life was forever transformed as I sat in every one of his theology classes. The best lesson in theology and holy love, I learned from Dr. Bill Ury, was demonstrated not only by the way he took me in as a foreign student but how he and

I worked a very menial cleaning job to make ends meet while he was professor. I knew him as "my big teacher" as I learned how to teach a class of adult Sunday school at Christ United Methodist Church, Jackson, Mississippi. Bill introduced me to great Christian minds, and I call myself a most privileged African minister to have sat under some of their feet and learned more of triune love.

What amazed me, nevertheless, through all my academic journey and ministerial journey I have never found a heart and a brain so profound in biblical truth and humble as I did in Dr. Bill Ury. He benefitted so much from his teachers, but he found his own God-given unique way of expressing and living out practically very rich depths of God's love and grace. Bill has passionately ministered this love around the world, including in my own country of Kenya. May God continue to use him to drink from the deep springs of God's love and to share these unsearchable treasures to His people.

Essay

Whether you sit in his seminary classes, Sunday school classes, holiness camp meetings, conferences, or church sermons, interrelated themes of self-giving love, sacrificial love, other-oriented, selflessness, always ring through Bill Ury's messages and teachings. It is his most marvelous hermeneutical way of unlocking the biblical narrative and trinitarian theology of "holy love." In an age of less theological reflection in relation to the practicalities of missions, Ury provides deep thoughts on how to take what could remain speculative doctrine of the Trinity to practical applications in missions. But his thoughts are more than practical applications, they are indeed the logical understanding of the nature of the Trinity as missional.

It may not be easy sifting through modern missionary literature to find any serious engagement of the Trinity in missions. But the more one gets into understanding the hermeneutics of the Holy Trinity, the more one unlocks two conjoined twins within it: the sanctifying love of God tied to the self-giving Spirit of missions. This is, perhaps, the tragedy of a world that is becoming more and more secular and distanced from its theological and sacred origins. In early Christianity, theological discussions were within the realm of the marketplace of ideas. That is why the Church saved civilization by protecting its culture and art and by humanizing the world through giving it the right concept of "personhood" as articulated to us so well by Bill Ury. The ultimate worth of human person, which becomes part of the motivating factor in reaching to the uttermost parts of the earth, cannot be understood without its divine origins. When a United Nations Secretary General talks of the sanctity of human life, he is basically affirming a gift that the Church gave the world. Bill Ury's groundbreaking dissertation on *Trinitarian Personhood* is a marvelous research and exploration on this reality.

Trinitarian Missions

Christian missions in classical theology has not been known as tangential to the Church, but as definitive of its very essence. The Church is God's mission to the world. This is God's initiative, rooted in His initiative to restore and heal Creation through the sent agency of the Church.* John D. Zizioulas, who has spent significant effort

---

* Darrell L. Gruder, ed. *Missional Church: A Vision for the Sending Church in North*

in trying to understand the Church's way of "being as communion," discussed the relationship between "Ministry and Communion" by asserting that ministry is "initiated by the Father who actually sends the Son in order to fulfill and realize the eternal design of the Holy Trinity to draw man and Creation to participation to God's very life."[*] The Holy Spirit, as the third person of the Holy Trinity, has a role in this economy in that there is "the interdependence between ministry and the concrete community of the Church as the latter is brought about by *the koinonia* of the Spirit."[†]

It is the "indwelling Trinity that makes Him 'a god by adoption and grace.... The inner presence of the Trinity, like a magnet draws man's conscious attention..." In his "Treatise on The Least of the Commandments,*" Symeon, The New Theologian*, examined the fact that the Holy Trinity is not only a treasure we possess, but that we are adopted and possessed by God through the Triune reality which "unites us to Himself and makes us cleave to Himself."[‡] This is what *Divine Conspiracy* says in faith "we rest ourselves upon the reality of the Trinity" and thus get "enmeshed in the true world of God."[§]

T. A. Noble stated that "the heart surely of Christocentric and therefore Trinitarian basis for the Wesleyan doctrine of Christian holiness as perfect love" is rooted in the Cappadocian understanding of trinitarian holiness. This doctrine was basically the revivalist doctrine of the evangelical circles of the eighteenth and the nineteenth century. It is possible to see then that, while those two centuries may not have

---

America (Grand Rapids: Eerdmans, 1998), 4.

[*]   John Zizioulas, *Being as Communion: Studies in Personhood and the Church*, (Crestwood, NY: St. Vladimir's Seminary Press, 1997), 211.

[†]   Zizioulas, *Being as Communion*, 212.

[‡]   *Symenon The New Theologian: The Discourses*, translated by C. J. de Cantanzaro (New York: The Missionary Society of St. Paul, 1980), 35 and 288.

[§]   Dallas Willard, *The Divine Conspiracy: Discovering Our Hidden Life in God* (San Francisco: HarperCollins, 1998), 318.

been the best in trinitarian reflection, it was this period that the holy character of God informed the self-giving sacrificial nature of the emergent missionary movement.[*] It is not a surprise that after the revivalist era of John Wesley, who taught and articulated to the world sanctification as perfect love and who died in 1791, the first Protestant mission agency, Baptist Missionary Society, was founded exactly a year later in 1792 by William Carey. This is not mere coincidence, but an indication that the ultimate divine love preached by Wesley begets ultimate divine commitment in missions as espoused by Carey.

Communicative Love

One of the greatest mysteries and dynamisms of love is communication. Love is never silent. It is ever giving, and it is ever going. When talking of the Trinity, the late Dr. Dennis F. Kinlaw, one of the leading thinkers in the holiness movement, saw that "perichoresis and *agape* love can only be understood in terms of interrelatedness of persons." Out of this argument, Kinlaw established that in missions, Christians "must lose their lives in something and for someone(s) beyond themselves". He stated that in reality "the pagan world is filled with data". to support that *agape* love, which is a manifestation of trinitarian relationship, supports the principle of giving oneself for someone else.[†] The concept of love, sharing, and communication, informed Kinlaw's thinking when he expressed, "Love is His inner life, the divine life, which the three persons of the blessed Trinity co-inherently share." God's love communicates because by nature the dynamism of love cannot

---

[*] T. A. Noble, "The Cappadocians, Augustine and Trinitarian Holiness," 35th Annual Meeting of Wesleyan Theological Society, Azusa Pacific University, March 3-4, 2000, 19.
[†] Kinlaw, *Let's Start With Jesus* (Wilmore, KY: The Francis Asbury Society, 2005), 134.

allow it to keep quiet.

Communication is an essential element in missions. Missionaries have historically struggled to have their message understood. They are, therefore, the respected preservers of human language and culture. As a matter of fact, some of the missionary failures are related to attempts to safeguard the integrity of the gospel as communicated in a foreign context. Even when human language became inadequate, the Triune God has always come in as their aid to make sense, in the purest divine language, what missionaries intended to communicate. That is why in every culture where the gospel has been shared, deep theological truths are understood even by people with the most basic education.

When God communicates, He is creative.* This is what produces missions. No wonder then, that it has always been those movements that are characterized by triune piety: the monastics, the pietists, the Puritans, the Methodists, the holiness revivalists, and the Pentecostal movements in their times have been the keenest in the missionary enterprise. These movements have been structured along "loose fellowship" formats that render the communicative nature of the Triune Love easily shared at home and in other parts of the world. This is because the ultimate expression of the full life of God in a person subsequently leads to the ultimate sacrifice in missions — *My Utmost for His Highest,* as Oswald Chambers, the missionary to Egypt, would put it.

It is within a selfless and non-egotistic environment where commitment to God becomes commitment to His mission in the world. That is to say, the more one is at "the disposal of God, the Church, and his neighbor, the more his heart is open to the needs

---

* Dennis F. Kinlaw, *Let's Start with Jesus,* 28-32.

of others" in missions.* Christian faith is intrinsically missionary because the dynamism within the Trinity carries with it the unveiling of that truth and love to the world. Missions is about God's self-communication as He establishes relationship with the world. So as theology is the queen of the sciences, "mission is the mother of theology."

Brother's Keeper

The human sense of mission and being a "brother's keeper" began as a process of reflection of this image in a world where Adam and Eve were created to tend and subdue. The first two chapters of Genesis demonstrate this amazing harmony between God and His creatures, and especially between Adam and his Creator. Adam understood his mission very well, to "be fruitful and fill the earth and subdue it." Even when God gave his "special mission," that of loving and caring for Eve, he knew it perfectly well. This perfect love was confirmed when Adam said those best words of love ever uttered by man: "This is bone of my bones and flesh of my flesh; she shall be called woman, because she was taken out of man." As a matter of fact, God did not add any more adjectives to Adam's description of Eve but to say that man has no other duty except to leave his father and mother and be joined to his wife. The nakedness and the absence of shame is a sign of their purity, innocence, and openness before each other and before God.

The next time we hear an encounter between God and Adam, the latter's language has changed. First, God said to him "Where are

---

* See Stephen Ackermann, "The Church as Person in the Theology of Hans Urs Von Balthasar," *Communion: International Catholic Review* 29 (Summer 2002), 245.

you?" Did God really not know where Adam was? He knew. I think the biggest lesson here is that Adam was there physically, but he was spiritually dead. He was as far from his Creator as anything can be. The relationship was broken. It was broken vertically (love for God disappears with vital piety) and thus the first horrible utterances of a sinner in history: "I was afraid." The relationship was broken horizontally for love for neighbor, love for missions disappears with waning love for God. Thus, the blame game, "The woman you gave to be with me." Because of sin, the breaking of this love relationship, and loss of vital holiness, catastrophic things happened. Adam was cursed. Eve was cursed. The serpent and the ground (Creation) were cursed. The end result was the most devastating disharmony. When we lose relationship with Him, we lose holiness. When we lose holiness, we lose our sense of mission. Yes, we lose even our sense of our first mission to the family. Whatever social work we attempt to do in this state, family or beyond, often becomes selfish and destructive.

This Adamic loss is echoed through Adam's sons. It is noticeable that before Cain murdered his brother, God knew that the sin problem was already inherent in his nature, even before the act. In Genesis 4:6 God asked him, "Why are you angry?" The second question that faced him (almost like his father, save that it was about another person) was "Where is your brother?" His answer was no different from that of his father earlier, running from responsibility, "Am I my brother's keeper?" Adam's dual mission of tending God's Creation, and particularly His special creation Eve, had collapsed with that of his holy relationship with his God. Cain, an elder brother's mission of being his brother's keeper had collapsed with his murderous anger. Love for brethren, as God loves, in word and deed, is inherent to the mission of the church.

This brother's keeper imperative is demonstrated as possible by many who had experienced radical love throughout the Scriptures, even in the worst of situations. Abraham was purified from idolatry toward the son of his old age and he became a blessing to the nations. Noah was a righteous man and he engaged in the mission of building the ark to redeem what remained of humans and God's creation in his generation. Moses had to remove his Egyptian Pharaonic "sandals," standing on holy ground by the burning bush, so he could be sent back on a mission to rescue the children of Israel. Isaiah was touched by the angelic tongs for his lips to be cleansed so he could say, "Here I am, send me." Paul was made an instrument of the gospel to the Gentiles and kings when he met Jesus face-to-face, while on a murderous mission to Damascus, and he parted with his pharisaical pride.

Great Commission and Great Commandment

It is no surprise that the passage we have come to know as the Great Commission, combines both the dynamic process of disciple-making with a triune baptismal formula (Matthew 28:19). This is not an accidental addendum, but an intricate ground for our Christian witness. As a matter of fact, the Christian church took this dual mandate seriously through history. The Great Commission became the basis for evangelization and discipleship, as well as baptizing and incorporating people into the Church in the triune name of God.

Most of us depend on this first gospel account of the Great Commission for missional mandate. When we look, however, at John 3:16, a well-known verse in Christian circles, the triune missionary dictates are very clear. John affirmed great trinitarian ontological statements when he wrote "For God so loved the world that He gave His one and only Son, that whoever believes in Him shall not perish but have eternal life." The *cosmos* implied in the book of John is connected to the One known as discipling all *ethnos* in the gospel of Matthew. The concept of love so pertinent to missionary drive and its usage in this Johannine Scripture is indicative of the perichoretic interpenetration within the Triune Reality as a source of missions.

Missions in simple language is a byproduct of love within the Father, Son, and the Holy Spirit. That God "gave His only Son" affirms a missionary idea of "sending," as a fruit of love within that Triune Reality. "That whosoever believes", does not only point to the universality of the missionary message, but affirms that the establishment of "relationship" based on the veracity of the gospel is an entrance into the triune life of God. The Scripture ends with having eternal life. This means the relationship is not perishable and is eternal because it is established by "undying" reciprocal love.

In the community of the saints, "love is forever given and forever enjoyed…the love of God is actually tested and known."* This also carries the inevitable idea that Christian testimony arises out of a triune reality which recognizes that

> Jesus manifested a relationship of unbroken love and obedience to the one He called the Father, a love and obedience sustained by the unfailing love and faithfulness of that Father; and those who believe and follow have been enabled through the presence of the Spirit actually to participate in this shared life of

---

* Leslie Newbigin, *The Open Secret: An Introduction to Theology of Mission* (Grand Rapids, Eerdmans, 1995), 149.

mutual love, which is the being of the Trinity.[*]

The relational aspects of a loving Father and the idea of sending is seen in the Father's giving of the Son. The fourth gospel also testifies that the beginning of the mission of the Son in the world, with the company of heaven and full authority and pleasure, was marked by a trinitarian witness, love, and affirmation. John declared, "Look, the Lamb of God, who takes away the sin of the world .... I saw the Spirit come down from heaven as a dove and remain on Him" (John 1:29, 32). The Gospel of Luke adds, "And a voice came from heaven; 'You are my Son, whom I love; with You I am well pleased." (Luke 3:22).

So Send I You

One of the most powerful missionary statements in the Gospel of John is John 20:21 where Jesus says, "As the Father sent Me, I am sending you." The implication is that the mission is a triune mission. From that center, the mission comes to the incarnate Christ, and subsequently from Him it comes to us through the power of the Holy Spirit. This "sending" missionary understanding of the divine enables us to conceptualize why "God sen[t] . . . His Son into the world" (John 3:17), and why "the Counselor comes, whom I will send to you from the Father" (John 15:26) as Jesus put it. It is within this context that we understand well the trinitarian economy that Bill Ury refers to as "the activity of the Father, Son, and Holy Spirit" or "a community where the implication of our personhood is worked out."[†] There is a mutual obedience and submission also

---

[*] Newbigin, *The Open Secret*, 89.
[†] M. William Ury, *Trinitarian Personhood: Investigating the Implications of a Relational*

expressed in Johannine literature (John 14:26).

Luke records that Jesus made reference to the Father sending Him in the power of the Holy Spirit in Luke 4:17-18. The scroll of the prophet Isaiah was handed to Him. Unrolling it, He found the place where it is written: "The Spirit of the Lord is on Me, because He has anointed Me to preach good news to the poor." It was also in the context of the return of the seventy-two that Jesus underscored the interconnectedness of the Triune Reality in the redemption of the world. In Luke 10:21-22, the text reads thus:

> At that time Jesus, full of joy through the Holy Spirit, said, "I praise You, Father, Lord of heaven and earth, because You have hidden these things from the wise and learned, and revealed them to little children. Yes, Father, for this was Your good pleasure. All things have been committed to Me by my Father. No one knows who the Son is except the Father, and no one knows who the Father is except the Son and those to whom the Son chooses to reveal Him.

In expositing this passage Samuel Escobar has argued that: "This is one of those passages in the Gospels that has both a missionary as well as a trinitarian thrust, because the biblical foundation of mission is trinitarian, which explains why great movements of missionary advance are born in the cradle of spiritual revival."*

Dr. Robert K. Lang'at, Bishop of the Africa Gospel Church-Kenya, was

---

Definition (Eugene OR: Wipf and Stock Publishers, 2002), 280.
* Samuel Escobar, *The New Global Mission: The Gospel from Everywhere to Everyone* (Intervarsity Press: Downer's Grove, 2003), 95.

born on June 3, 1967 in Kenya. He's married to Dr. Jane C. Lang'at and blessed with four children. He is an alumnus of Kenya Highlands University, Asbury University, Wesley Biblical Seminary, and Drew University. He has served as a pastor in a number of congregations in Kenya, Assistant Academic Dean at Wesley Biblical Seminary, and Professor of Theology and Provost at Kabarak University; has chaired a number of ministry boards including: Tenwek Hospital, Christian Health Association of Kenya, and Mission for Essential Drugs and Supplies. He also serves on the Board of World Gospel Mission, Kabarak University, and is previously board member of Evangelical Alliance of Kenya. Has published in various journals, including Methodist History, Evangelical Review of Theology, A Journal of Salvation Army Theology and Ministry, Africa Journal of Evangelical Theology, *and in* Global Wesleyan Dictionary of Theology.

CHAPTER FOURTEEN

Holy Love and the Nuptial Metaphor of Scripture

Diane N. Ury

Tribute

During an interview for a position as "evangelist", I was asked how I handled the Pauline passages about women's roles in the church. I replied that I have no issue. My husband has told me to teach, to preach, and to be ordained. So, I have. For 38 years we have lived within the nuptial mystery, "union of distinction." Female and male, small town girl most at home in the woods, and large Asian city boy at home in any part of the world. Our mutual receiving of one another regularly gave me unlimited access to one of the finest hearts and minds on triune personhood. I will always personally believe that Bill Ury is the best classroom teacher of theology. His classes expanded my entire being when he was my professor. All my adult life Bill has seen me in ways I never would have. His unrelenting, no-ceiling, "Yes, do it", to every whisper of an idea I ever had is the rich soil out of which I've lived and grown. He has always protected my person by encouraging my intellect while at the same time honoring the incalculable worth of my call to motherhood. We can't even distinguish our dreams for life — was that mine or his? Our persons have formed one another. As William Booth seriously listened to Catherine's mind and heart, he opened every gate for her to proclaim the depths of the gospel. The Booth's marriage sets a marvelous example of mutual holy love. Serving together with my husband as Ambassadors for Holiness enfleshes our marriage. Best of all, as I ride on his brilliant coattails through life, I get to hear Bill Ury expound on his ever-growing understanding of holy love which comes forth from his worship of the triune God.

Essay

The message of the Bible, the mystery of the gospel, is that the triune God intends to live with human persons in intimate, mutual, face-to-Face union.[*] That was our created reality, it remains the intention of the heart of God, and is the essence of biblical salvation — union with God, the life of God in the soul and in the body of human persons. Christianity becomes distorted and weak when we think our story begins in Genesis 3. It does not begin with

---

[*] "…that they may all be one; even as You, Father, are in Me and I in You, that they also may be in Us." John 17:21.

the Fall or with sin. Our story begins with a wedding and offers life everlasting in faithful union with holy love. The revelation of reality also pivots at a wedding and culminates with the marriage of the Lamb and His bride.

This essay is an invitation to explore the nature of holy love expressed in Scripture through the nuptial metaphor of God's relationship with human persons. This realization is essential to comprehending full salvation, the meaning of human existence, human sexuality, and a theology of intimacy.

The Nuptial Metaphor

A metaphor is a means of communicating a reality through a word picture or symbol. It is not a simile which says something is "like" or "as" something else. A metaphor is not merely a comparison of resemblance between two things. Rather it is saying, "This is that."* The union of divine Persons within the Triune God of holy love is the source from which human marriage becomes the symbol.

One of the greatest issues facing the American Church is an impoverished imagination.† If a sacrament is a physical reality which conveys spiritual mystery, biblical metaphor is God-breathed language which conveys spiritual mystery.‡ Let's not miss it.

Nuptial means wedding and marriage. It signifies the ideas of

---

* Dennis Kinlaw, *Lectures in Old Testament Theology* (Anderson, Indiana: Francis Asbury Press, 2010), 442.

† Phil Vischer, Host, "Beth Moore's Exit & the Problem of "Impoverished Imaginations" with Karen Swallow Prior", Holy Post Podcast #448, 17 March 2021. https://www.holypost.com/post/episode-448-beth-moore-s-exit-the-problem-of-impoverished-imaginations-with-karen-swallow-prior .

‡ Malcom Guite, *Waiting on the Word* (London, UK: Canterbury Press, 2015), 147-150. I won't take time here to give full expression to the relationship of metaphor, insights, and sacrament. Reading this passage impacted my thoughts. Also, C.S. Lewis believed Christianity is God expressing Himself through real things.

covenant, vows, promise, and faithfulness. Primarily, its meaning implies faithful union and oneness. "Union" inherently implies two distinct entities coming together.

God reveals Himself as Husband who has always intended us to live in unbroken intimacy and belonging with Him — the picture of marriage (Jeremiah 31:31-32, Ezekiel 16). Biblical history is seen primarily in nuptial categories[*] because God reveals His holy love through making covenants.[†] Redemptive history is God continuously offering His personal Presence, to restore communion with and to sanctify His beloved (John 14-17). He came to His people, proposed to her, rescued her, brought her to Himself, made mutual vows with her, moved in to live with her (tabernacle/temple), took on her nature (Incarnation), bore her sins and death, forgave her, raised her to life, cleansed her, took her into His triune life (Ascension), and lives within her (Pentecost). Throughout this covenant union comes fruitfulness. (Genesis 12-17, Exodus 19-20, 20, 36; John 15; Ephesians 5:21-33; 1 Corinthians 6:19).

In ways the legal or familial metaphors cannot fulfill, the nuptial metaphor reveals God's inexorable passion for, delight in, and devotion to His creatures. Every time the Creator says, "I will be your God and you shall be My people... I will never leave you or forsake you... you are Mine," these are nuptial promises of belonging. He intends to re-create us.[‡]

---

[*]   Dennis F. Kinlaw, *Let's Start with Jesus* (Grand Rapids, Michigan: Zondervan, 2005), 57-64.

[†]   ANE cultures employed covenants. But perhaps covenants are a human symbol of the transcendent self-offering, *hesed* nature of the triune God's nuptial view toward all of His creation.

[‡]   We are familiar with scriptural metaphors employing legal, kingdom, and familial categories in which we learn God as Judge, King, and Father; our salvation as justification, deliverance, adoption and regeneration. However, the over-arching theme of the Bible is the nuptial metaphor which conveys the mutual and complete self-giving in face-to-Face oneness, resulting in exchanged life and transformation of character to God's likeness.

What does it truly mean to be a whole and flourishing human person? Fullness of human ontology is to live in union with God, oneness like a marriage that transforms us.*

Triune Nature

Primary to revelation, is the eternal one true living God Himself. He is Trinity — three distinct Persons in union. The triune essence is mutual, other-oriented, self-offering, and receiving. Each of the three distinct divine Persons eternally are oriented outside of themselves, toward one another in mutual love. "To be a person is to be oriented toward someone beyond oneself."† The New Testament word for love, *agape*, contains this other-oriented meaning. *Agape* love is the holy essence of the triune God.

The Trinity's creative act flows out of His self-offering nature of love. Created human personhood, in His image contains this relational essence (Genesis 1:26-27). To be a person is to be in relationship. That fundamental reality is true in God before it is true in human persons.‡ We are created with need for intimate relationship and belonging, primarily with God Himself, secondarily with other people.

---

* "...so you may attain to fullness of being, the fullness of God Himself." Eph. 3:19.
† Dennis Kinlaw, *We Live as Christ* (Nappanee, Indiana: Francis Asbury Press, 2001), 56.
‡ M. William Ury, *Trinitarian Personhood: Investigating the Implications of a Relational Definition* (Eugene, Oregon: Wipf and Stock Publishers, 2001) In this work resides some of the most complete discussion and research ever compiled on the development of relational trinitarian thought. Out of this work I have read and heard Bill Ury make this statement countless times.

Nature of Revelation

The Bible itself reflects God's triune nature because it is God's personal, loving offer of Himself, initiating relationship with humans using human language, inviting our response.* In this way God enters our world to create relationship with us. We must read the Bible's revelation about the way to walk with Him as human persons, including our sexuality, not merely as "behavior management." It is God pursuing us; it's the doorway into the mystery of human experience with God's nature of holy love. God is inviting us to live in personal communion with Him so that He can restore us to the joy and fullness we were intended to experience when we live according to His ways† (John 15:9-11). The form and content of Scripture itself is nuptial — a "union of distinction" of God's breath with human language (2 Tim. 3:16).

God's personal triune nature is "union of distinction", a "wedding" of distinct divine Persons. The nuptial reality I'm identifying in Scripture is the "union of distinction" of divinity with human person.‡ God initiates union between Himself and the

---

* I had the privilege of being taught by Dr. Gary Cockerill in biblical studies and Greek. This was his view of how we as students are to understand approaching Scripture.

† A biblical understanding of human sexuality is essentially contingent within the nuptial metaphor. The scope of this essay cannot address sexuality in particular, but one must see the critical need to comprehend its nature in relationship to the nuptial reality. Also see Christopher West, *Our Bodies Tell God's Story* (Grand Rapids, Michigan: Brazos Press, 2020) for a compelling expression of human sexuality understood within the nuptial metaphor.

‡ A brief perusal of the nuptial view of the biblical narrative will show this recurrent theme is the story of full salvation. The distinct triune Persons of the Godhead manifest "union of distinction" in: the Bible — divine with human language; Sabbath/seventh Day — divine with time and space; Humanity — divine breath in human dust; the Law — divine character with human behavior; Prophets — divine word with human voice; Incarnation — the fully divine and fully human Second Person of the Trinity; Ascension — union of human nature within Triune godhead; Pentecost/The Church — divine in union with sanctified human persons; The Return — divine Son in everlasting union with human Church, His Body, at the final marriage supper of the Lamb. (This hermeneutic assists with a biblical understanding of human heterosexual marriage.)

human race. He creates humans in His image, a union of dust and divinity, intended for intimate love with Him. What we call "the Fall" was a cosmic event of unfaithfulness. Adultery. A distrust in God's character, a separation and divorce from our Source to belong only to ourselves, not to God. The whole narrative of the rest of the Bible contains God's pursuit of a way to restore His creatures back to His original intention: faithful union and belonging with Himself.

Creation

The climax of creation occurred on the seventh day with a wedding.[*] God freely chose to enter personally into time and space, making that day holy because His personal presence abides there.[†] In a real sense God wed Himself to the realm of His beloved creation.[‡] He took the dust into His hands, intimately forming a human body, brought it to His face and breathed *nephesh*, His own life, into the created matter.[§] That union of divine with human flesh is what

---

[*]   Kinlaw, *Let's Start with Jesus*, 41.

[†]   Neil B. MacDonald, *Metaphysics and the God of Israel: Systematic Theology of the Old and New Testaments* (Grand Rapids: Baker Academic Books, 2006), 79-87. "Covenant (*berith*) is the OT term for the basic relationship between the God of Israel — Yahweh — and His people, the people of Israel. (Barth defines covenant as: 'the historical reality with which the OT is concerned whether it actually uses the word or not: "I will be your God and you will be My people."'" MacDonald says covenant exists because of "God's self-determination to become the sanctifier of His personal relationship with humankind, which first occurred on the "7th Day". Ibid., 96. His metaphysical systematic is dependent upon the cruciality of God's acts of creation on the "7th Day". Also, Kinlaw, *Let's Start with Jesus*, 38-39. "If anything else possesses any holiness, it is because of its association with Him.... because God, the Holy One, is present."

[‡]   Kinlaw, *Let's Start with Jesus*, 69.

[§]   I'm aware that I will be thought naive, at the very least, for believing this actually happened. But I'm also aware that those who dismiss this as "merely poetry" or myth have a dangerously inadequate Christology, anthropology, and soteriology. If this is impossible, so is the Incarnation, and we are all without hope.

created a living person. Without His breath in our bodies no one is fully alive as a human person*(Rom. 8:1-17, 12:2; Eph. 4:13; Phil. 3:9-12; Col. 3:1-4).

The Creator is distinct from the created world. He alone is uncreated. We call that "transcendence" — ontologically other in substance and quality, impossible to manipulate. Transcendent "otherness" is not spatial geography. It's a qualitative essence statement. We must be careful about only defining "holiness" as "separate." God is imminent holiness: personally present goodness, righteousness, compassion, truth, justice, and love. "Holy" includes the self-offering immanence of triune "holy love", therefore His shared life with humans was the beginning of the nuptial story of "union of distinction", Creator with creature, in perfection of intimacy. Genesis 2 reveals the consummation of our reality. Human persons are created to live in wedded intimacy with the Holy One, in oneness.

God Completes Us

To consummate means "to bring to completion or perfection."† The climactic wedding on the seventh day was not the marriage of Adam and Eve, but the wedding, completion, perfection of God in intimate union with those created in His image, those with the capacity to bear the presence of God in their entire beings, body and spirit (1 Thessalonians 5:23-24).‡

---

* People can be biologically alive, but not fully human persons as God intends. They are "lost" because their beings are empty of the personal presence of the One who is *zoe*, true Life (1 John 5:12).

† No marriage is considered valid without sexual union of distinction — "consummating" is the wedding. The theological origin of this consistent sociological mores is Gen. 2:1-7.

‡ Diane N. Ury, "A Comparison of Abraham J. Heschel's Concept of Sabbath as Bride

By His intentional design, we are created with longings, hunger, and desire. To be incomplete, God declared to be *tov méod,* "very good, exactly as I intended." To be a perfect human person is to *not* be complete in oneself.* Like the Trinity, human marriage is a "union of distinction" — male and female.† Adam and Eve bear that image of triune life as Eve is *ezer* (helper) *kenegdo* (suitable) with Adam. *Kenegdo* means corresponds to, is equal to, adequate to, and being "before your face."‡

When we focus too much on human marriage as the symbol of Triune reality, we're skewing things off center. It is a symbol (Ephesians 5:21-32), which is critical, essential to human society. But it is not the primary reality. The nuptial reality is individual persons' union with God. Human marriage will only reflect triune holy love when each individual husband and wife is personally "a complete person, to the measure of the stature which belongs to the fullness of Christ" (Ephesians 4:13).

Unmarried persons equally reflect triune holy love as they live their "new self" of union with Christ, in their context of mutual self-offering and receiving with other persons in "the church, which is His body, the fullness of Him who fills all in all" (Ephesians 1:22).

Marriage, or any other form of unity among people, is

---

and Dennis Kinlaw's Concept of the Nuptial Metaphor" (Master's Thesis, Wesley Biblical Seminary, 2008). Here you will find a fuller treatment of the relationship of the seventh day to the nuptial metaphor.

* Kinlaw, *We Live as Christ.* 56-57. Also, Dennis F. Kinlaw, *"Holiness and Human Sexuality,"* Wesley Biblical Seminary 2007 *Chamberlain Holiness Lectures* (pre-published manuscript: 2007), 8-9. Kinlaw describes how every human is not self-originating, self-sustaining, self-explanatory, or self-fulfilling.

† Sexual difference in sexual intercourse and marriage is not a random imposition; it is the symbolic representation of God's triune nature, and of God's nature in union with our nature. It is an icon/symbol of the deep mystery of the intention of our creation. To be made as sexual beings is to be made as men and women with a desire for union. Union of distinction in sexual intercourse is the created intention of God.

‡ Dennis F. Kinlaw *"Holiness and Human Sexuality,"* Lecture 2, 14.

dependent, first of all upon our being one with the life of the Trinity, receiving Jesus' character of glory, and Jesus' life within ours (John 17:21-23).

"Our attachment to Christ is the single *necessary* relationship in our lives. Any necessary human relationship will eventually corrupt our ethics. When any other attachment threatens that primary commitment to Him, all of our relationships are blighted."*

Intimate human relationships are integral to human flourishing. But the primary source of every human person's existence, the ultimate need we all have that is the core of our very good human nature, is to be intimately wed to our Creator. God completes us.† He is the full satisfaction of human existence. Regardless of one's marital status or sexual orientation, God's personal Presence in our flesh is our created intention. Surrendered, obedient, faithful union with God brings eternally more satisfaction than human sex or marriage can provide. Oneness with the Holy One will transform anyone into a person of holy love.

The created entities of the first six days of creation supply complementary, corresponding pairings in days one through six. Day seven is the pairing of the personal Presence of God with His image bearers. God is our Helper, *ezer* (Psalm 54:4; 124:8). He created us in His image, corresponding to Him. We are designed to live in mutually suitable, face to Face, cherished belonging with God Himself. We are assured of this when Jesus refers to the Holy Spirit as "Helper" (John 15:26-16:15).

This nuptial reality goes beyond legality and forgiveness.

---

* Dennis F. Kinlaw, *Preaching in The Spirit* (Nappanee, Indiana: Francis Asbury Press, 1985), 26-27.
† There's a reason Jerry Maguire's proclamation to Dorothy, "You complete me!", is so compellingly romantic. But it's merely the symbol of our true longing for God. We are made for Jesus. *Jerry Maguire*, directed by Cameron Crowe (Gracie Films, 1996).

Its purpose is oneness and likeness. That which was the created intention of God's heart for human persons, became the intention of our re-creation after the fall.

Incarnation

Like the Trinity, Jesus is "union of distinction." The Incarnation is the nuptial reality which is central to the gospel. The eternal Son of God has wedded Himself to His creation as the Son of Man. Within Christ's ontology, fully God and fully human, dwells the healing of the separation between God and humans.

> *The Creator of all,*
> *To repair our sad fall,*
> *From His heav'n stoops down,*
> *Lays hold of our nature, and joins to His own.*
>
> *Our Immanuel came,*
> *The whole world to redeem,*
> *And incarnated show'd*
> *That man may again be united to God!*

We are a ruined race due to our unfaithful broken union with God through sin. Jesus is the perfect union of natures which reconciles and restores us to God.

Atonement is nuptial. It refers not only to the cross; "*at-one-ment*" begins with the Incarnation.

In Genesis 2 God breathed His Spirit into the dust creating

---

* Charles Wesley, *Hymns for the Nativity of our Lord* (Madison, New Jersey: The Charles Wesley Society, 1991), 34.

union with human persons. Instead of Adam and Eve being the determiners for humanity, now the Spirit overshadows Mary, and God weds Himself to the humanity of Mary, the new Eve.[*] "He Himself likewise also partook of the same" (Heb. 2:14). Humans are conceived in sin, therefore from the moment of His conception the Second Adam begins to recapitulate, to re-create human existence by obediently, faithfully re-living the human race as He always intended it to be lived. Jesus is sinless because He never broke His union with the Trinity. Therefore, He has power to forgive and transform us.

God the Son became fully human to re-create humanity so that we all can be who we are created to be. The God Man not only justifies us, He regenerates and saves us by His life, restoring us to become new creatures of love and belonging to God, who by nature obey Him and walk in His ways[†] (Romans 5:9-11). He took our fallen human nature and brought God's image into it once again, denouncing the curse of the fall (Romans 5:12-21). He will write His own name of Holy Love, His law upon our hearts and minds through our union with Him (2 Corinthians 2-6).

We are saved by His entire life, from conception through the ascension, and into Pentecost. Jesus is our salvation (Luke 2:26-38).

Christian Perfection

Shalem is the Hebrew word for complete. It means to make full, to satisfy, to make whole, to perfect; finished; peace. In the New

---

[*] St. Irenaus, *Against Heresies* (Lib. 5, 19, 1:20, 2; 21,1: SC 153), 248-250, 260-264. Irenaeus understood Mary's trust and surrender to God as the recapitulation of Eve's distrust and unfaithful rebellion against God.
[†] *Lesslie Newbigen, Truth and Authority in Modernity* (Valley Forge, Pennsylvania: Trinity Press International, 1996) 38-39.

Testament its corresponding word is *teleos*, which means finished; lacking nothing necessary to completeness; perfect; to consummate.

In the beginning, before the Fall, human persons were perfect in our dependence upon and union with God and one another. I believe this is what is meant by "perfection" in the Bible. The New Testament call to perfection or completion is the same voice of the triune God walking in the Garden declaring, "This is very good, exactly what I intended." Jesus prays, "that they may be *perfected* into one, that the world may know that You sent Me, and loved them" (John 17:23). *Teteleiomenoi* (perfected) means "reaching the goal, to complete, to consummate, to raise to the state befitting him."* This is the triune God's eternal design and heart for every person, beginning in Genesis 1 when He declared our nature in union with Him to be *tov*.

"Christian perfection" is a life of complete dependence upon and union with God, issuing forth God's holy love for all people. The nuptial biblical concept of perfection does not focus upon our behavior: are we naughty or nice? Biblical perfection means finding our completeness in God alone. It is face to Face oneness with God — an intimate, mutual relationship of love in which we continuously breathe in His living breath. It is not merely a stage of spiritual growth.

To live holy lives is to be dependent upon the indwelling Christ, to be transformed by His glory, and to be drawn into the life of the Trinity. Jesus makes the Father's name known "so that the love with which You loved Me may be in them, and I in them" (John 17:26). Before holiness is "power over sin", holiness is holy love. Our holy, loving behavior flows out of loving union with triune holy love (1

---

* *Thayers Greek Lexicon, electronic database 2011, Biblesoft, Inc.*

John 4:16-17).

To experience full human personhood is to be wed to God. Only believing correct doctrine is not enough. We can get all A's in theology class and still suffocate, void of His breath. We can still be mean as snakes. God is our life. Our role is to help every kind of person into this depth of intimacy with Jesus. Then He can speak to them, convict them of sin, draw them to Himself, bring them to surrender, obedience, belonging and create holiness of heart and life.

Jesus is our Bridegroom, not only because He is coming back to take us as His bride, but because He, the Lord and Creator of the universe, once again wed Himself to our humanity in the Incarnation. He is forever bone of our bone, and flesh of our flesh! As the divine human being He took our sin and disaster, our wounds and brokenness right into His flesh, shed His blood for our sinfulness, destroyed all the devil's work on the Cross and set us free "at the consummation of the ages" (Heb. 9:26). When Christ returns, only those who now live in face-to-Face intimacy with Him will be those eagerly awaiting Him (Heb. 9:28). Those with faces He recognizes through unveiled intimacy will not have the door shut on them as He says to the unfamiliar, "Depart from Me, I never knew you" (Matt. 25:1-13).

This day, and for eternity Jesus Christ reigns on His Throne in heaven as the divine human being, interceding in perfect understanding on our behalf.

> "God in all His fullness was pleased to live in Christ, and by Him God reconciled everything to Himself. He made peace with everything in heaven and on earth by means of His blood on the cross. This includes you who were once so far away from God. You were His

enemies, separated from Him by your evil thoughts and actions, yet now He has brought you back as His friends. He has done this through His death on the cross in His own human body. As a result, He has brought you into the very presence of God, and you are holy and blameless as you stand before Him without a single fault. ...In Christ the fullness of God lives in a human body, and you are *complete* through your *union* with Christ. He is the Lord over every ruler and authority in the universe" (Colossians 1:19-22; 2:9-10 NLT).

My heart melts at the love of Jesus,
my brother, bone of my bone, flesh of my flesh,
married to me, dead for me, risen for me;

He is mine and I am His,
given to me as well as for me;
I am never so much mine as when I am His,
Or so much lost to myself until lost in Him;
*Then I find my true personhood.**

———————

Diane Nelson Ury is National Ambassador for Holiness with The Salvation Army USA. She is married to Bill Ury, has loved raising four children and cherishes their spouses and each of their children. She received a BA in Sociology from Asbury University and earned an MA in Theology from Wesley Biblical Seminary. Diane is an ordained elder in the Evangelical Methodist Church.

———————

* Arthur Bennett, ed. *Valley of Vision* (Edinburgh, Scotland: The Banner of Truth Trust, 1975) 44.

Acknowledgments

IT HAS BEEN a supreme honor to work with the essay contributors for this volume. Within a few hours of my presenting the idea and asking them if they'd like to participate in honoring Bill Ury with essays on holy love, every one of them accepted the opportunity. They are people of great character and love, whom I esteem greatly for their intellect and the way they live their lives. I thank each of you for adding this project to your very full lives, and for doing so with touching and admirable humility. Most of all I'm grateful to you for loving my husband.

Dr. Matt Friedeman graciously encouraged me to copy the format of a *festschrift* he had edited in 2017. I really liked his idea of the tribute accompanying the essay with a thematic prompt. He really liked the idea of a book honoring his good friend, Bill, and told me to go for it.

Dr. Becky Luman is so good at proof editing. As a former colleague and continual friend to us, I am so grateful she was on this team!

To the leadership of the Southern Territory of The Salvation

Army USA, I owe so much. Bill Ury has been a faithful partner and contributor to the theological training of the Army for decades. But it's difficult to articulate the mutual sense of family, faithful love and trust that is present here. Knowing Bill's passion for holy love, combined with his lifelong commitment to gathering together thinkers from various denominations to encourage one another in holiness, these leaders had the vision to see the value of a book like this. I shared my idea for including scholars from areas different than the Army along with Salvationist writers, and why this cross-fertilization among Christians committed to holy love is important for a Salvation Army publisher to support. They got it. They immediately said yes. And to this kind of willingness to provide fellowship, challenge and learning together, I say, "More, please."

I acknowledge you scores of individuals who would have loved to contribute to this *festschrift*, not because you want to publish your ideas, but because your life has been influenced by Bill Ury. It has pained me to know what could not happen in these limited pages. I ask your pardon.

Appendix

I AM FOREVER grateful to God for Dr. Bill Ury. When I joined Wesley Biblical Seminary in 2008, typical of anyone entering a new culture, I felt overwhelmed in many ways: new language, new food, and new ways of personal interactions. My first class was on systematic theology, that is how I met my first seminary professor, Dr. Ury. The concepts he taught were top notch; I had never heard several terminologies he mentioned in class. For the first time I heard words like: recapitulation, self-giving love, sanctification, Christology, just to name a few. As beautiful and exciting as it was learning these new concepts, nothing was more profound that to see it in real life. Dr. Ury, as I would regard him as a man after God's own heart modeled a self-giving, sanctified life. I was blessed to sit under a man who has untold wisdom and was ready and willing to share that wisdom. Interacting with Dr. Ury gave me an experience of God's unmatched grace to and for humanity. Dr. Ury intentionally spoke at a slower pace, so that I (and other international students) could understand what he taught. He went out of his way to help us understand the assignments and how it all fitted in both theory and practical. He opened his home to allow us to experience a home away from home. He stopped to greet us. He wanted to know people personally and could always give a listening ear. These traits I saw in Dr. Ury are priceless in my pastoral ministry. I remember his regular statement "being precedes doing." Relationships (healthy ones) are critical. People will be moved by how you bond with them before you can tell/do anything for them; it mirrors Christ's invitation to be consumed by His self-giving love first and foremost.

Agnes Ngeny Lang'at, Pastor
Living Word Africa Gospel Church
Kenya

Perichoresis. The Incarnation. Holylove. Personhood. Trinity.

A long time ago Dr. Ury introduced these, and many other truths, to me in seminary. A whole world of "holy love" wonder entered my life. They turned my ranch-style home Christianity into a gothic Cathedral where unimaginable beauty and mystery collided with the effervescent light of Holy Spirit's illumination and inspiration. I haven't worshipped, taught or preached the same way since.

I feel myself trying to impress Dr. Ury even now, writing as eloquently and succinctly as possible yet truthfully. I know it's silly but that is what happens when you encounter holy love. You want more.

As I am sitting at my dinner table tonight, I remember one dinner at his house 14 years ago and can't help but smile at the memory of Dr. Ury fielding questions from his kids about why swearing is bad. It was a constant going up and down an intellectual ladder of Dr. Ury bringing five syllable words and concepts down to everyday life…and it worked. The kids understood. It was a simple, yet unforgettable exercise in watching what happens when the almost gravitional pull of deep truths have taken hold of a man who in turn is able to not only understand them (as much as is possible) but also allow others to enter them. It's positively contagious.

That's what I have aspired to and tried to make of my ministry and my family life, succumb to the pull of God and His glorious truths of love and holiness and bring others along. For Dr. Ury's example of heart, mind and life I am eternally grateful and I only wish I could have studied under his wife as well. I have a feeling she would have outdone him, something we all aspired to do yet never could.

Andreas Kjernald, Pastor
United Methodist Church
Norway

It is difficult to put into words exactly how much Dr. Ury has shaped my life and ministry. His reputation preceded him as I went through college seeing him as a sort of theological titan. The first time I met him I asked him to sign my copy of his dissertation and was struck by his humility. Having the privilege to study under him in seminary, he helped strengthen the foundation of my faith. I found great joy in "being prepared to make a defense to anyone who asks you for a reason for the hope that is in you" (1 Peter 3:15). With gentleness and respect Dr. Ury passionately challenged my intellect. His demeanor in and out of the classroom, along with his comprehensive view of theology, has had lasting effects on my personal relationship with Jesus and on my ministry.

Daily I am reminded of concepts I learned from Dr. Ury. Ministering in Japan I have often found that people have given no thought to the nature of God. Dr. Ury's assertion that God is holy self-giving love is a truth that transforms hearts and minds around the world. I have also found that Christians here are under intense pressure to show the strength of their relationship with God by how much they do or how well they perform. Dr. Ury's balanced view that the nature of being and the nature of doing cannot be separated breathes fresh life into beleaguered Christians.

From allowing students to celebrate the Resurrection with his family at sunrise, to conscientiously taking notes at even the most basic sermon, Dr. Ury has lived out his theology in a way that is rarely seen. I am blessed beyond measure to have been trained by a man who so closely resembles his Savior.

Christina Blair Ito, Missionary
Koganei Tokyo Free Methodist Church
Tokyo, Japan

When I met Bill Ury as a first-year seminarian, I was in almost complete revolt against my Methodist/Holiness roots. But as I sat in Bill's lectures and learned to think more deeply about the nature of God, the tradition's reflection on Him, and the patterns of His work in the Incarnation and the Atonement, for the first time it all began to come together for me. But what struck me just as powerfully was not just what he taught, but how he taught it, with grace and humility and worship. I saw a profound confluence of message and messenger.

From Bill I learned the primacy of the personal, and that far from being a floating merely subjective and experiential category, such relationality takes on concrete form in the ethical content of the God of the Bible, who "gives what He commands." For me this is the heart of the gospel. As the Apostle Paul wrote, "The end of the commandment is love from a pure heart, and of a good conscience, and of a faith unfeigned." These insights have colored everything I have had to say in my years of pastoral ministry and have led me in worship of the Triune God, and the wonders of his holy love. Thank you, Bill, for giving me back my tradition, and for embodying the truth of your message. You have both lived and taught it well. The holy love of God is evident in your life and ministry. I owe you an eternal debt. Please know that you are loved and esteemed. Your work has not been in vain. May the Holy One bless and keep you and may His face shine upon you!

Your grateful student,
Rev. Matt Johnson, Pastor
Lost Creek Emmanuel Missionary Church
Hicksville, Ohio

What a treasure it has been that Bill Ury has shared his life with me. I guess we go back to the Sunday school class at CUMC. As I sat on the back row each week, little did I know what was happening and how my life would be molded by his faithful teaching from God's Word. Little did I know that all that discipleship talk would be the most important message I would ever hear. Because of Bill's pouring into me, I have tried to disciple my family, two different discipleship groups, and a Sunday school class. I can't count the times that I think about God's perfect plan (Master Plan of Discipleship) when

He used Al Coppedge and Bill's own sweet father to pour into him so him could pour into others like me, who could only attempt to pour into others as well, and to teach them to pour into others.

Bill has taught me so much, but if he had been unable to even utter a word, his ministry would have been just as effective because of the way he simply LOVES GOD and LOVES OTHERS. He taught me that Jesus said that was the greatest of all commandments. And he has done that so well!! To see the way he has loved Di, his kids, church family, strangers, enemies, has been a witness like none other.

I can count on one finger the one person that God has put in my life that best expresses the good news of the gospel as He would desire it to be so beautifully shared. And that is Bill Ury. I'm so grateful to God for using him to show me the love of Jesus through his life.

Scot Thigpen, CPA, CFP
President and Wealth Advisor, Thigpen Group
Madison, Mississippi

Every time I think of the concept of self-giving love, Dr. Ury and his family come to my mind. There has been an amazing consistency in his classroom, at his home and even through emails and Zoom that he is always giving himself to others. I am thankful that Dr. Ury has shown me what it means to live out the theology of holy love based on Triune perichoretic reciprocity. Although I am far from living that out like Dr. Ury, all of my ministry here in Japan is aiming at that holy love expressed in daily relationships with others.

It has been an honor to be a small part of his radio ministry,

Hour of Holiness. As I serve the Lord together with my wife in Tokyo, Japan, the weekly messages have been a refreshing water of life and holy love. Therefore, I am overjoyed that Dr. Ury has allowed me to lead the translation project of his book, *The Bearer.* People in Japan need to hear this message and I am thankful that we launched this book in February 2022.

As my wife and I raise three children, we pray that our children will grow up to be like the Ury children. In a world filled with false images and fake news, the legacy of Dr. Ury and Mrs. Diane is seen through their children. I am eternally thankful for what I learned in the classroom under Dr. Ury, and also what I experienced in interactions with him outside the classroom, even across the ocean. God has blessed me and many other Japanese students through Dr. Ury. Now the legacy is spreading all over the world. May the Lord continue to bless and use Dr. Ury to share His holy self-giving love. Amen, Amen, Amen.

Masato Ito, Pastor
Koganei Tokyo Free Methodist Church
Tokyo, Japan

It is hard to express in words the scope of my Uncle Bill's influence on my life. Long before I ever sat in his theology class at seminary and learned the Biblical basis of holy love, I was experiencing that love as his nephew. Ever since I was young, I have looked up to him, even before I fully knew why. He always had a way of making me feel like the most important person in the room and that his seeing me was the brightest part of his day. As I got older, I began immersing myself in his *Hour of Holiness* radio program, learning more about the love and holiness I had seen lived out so powerfully in his relationship with me and others. Little did I know that some of his CD's that I was listening to had been prepared by my future wife Tanya, who was then attending Wesley Biblical. And how appropriate that God brought her into my life within the context of one of his seminary classes, in which I was learning more about the biblical basis for holy love. Uncle Bill was there for me at every key stage of my life, first as a picture of holy love, then the explainer of holy love, and then the very means through which I began pursuing the one whom God destined for me to demonstrate (and receive) holy love. Every sermon I preach, and every life touched by our ministry carries along with it the lasting fragrance of Uncle Bill's life and ministry. And in these uncertain times, he has continued to be an anchor for me in my walk with Christ. I cannot thank Uncle Bill enough for what he has and continues to give me. He has all my love and admiration,

Cameron Ury, Pastor
Renton Park Chapel
Renton, WA

Recently I came across a working definition for joy, simply what someone experiences when someone else is glad to see or be with that person. The author went on to state that joy is always communicated through our faces. What stood out to me was the coupling of the relationship between experiencing joy and faces with 2 Corinthians 4:6. "For God, who said, 'Let there be light in the darkness,' has made this light shine in our hearts so that we know *the glory of God that is seen in the face of Jesus Christ.*" I have begun to wonder if that is what Advent is all about. In the Incarnation, God turned His holy, loving face towards us in joy — He gave us His attention and smiled because He was glad to be with us.

For me, the origins for such musings can be traced back to the influence of Dr. Bill Ury. Bill (if I may) embodies joy — he always smiles when he sees you; even under stress, Bill smiles because he values your face (and mine). And because he values Jesus' face, your face, and my face, every interaction, class, conversation, or prayer time is an endeavor to recognize the face of Jesus. Bill constantly looks for Jesus' face in every teaching opportunity, preaching occasion, Sunday school class, radio program, meal, or cup of coffee. "What light is Jesus' face bringing into this situation or to this person?"

I have experienced the face of Jesus Christ in and through Bill Ury's face. He has modeled for me, like Moses, that it is possible to know God face-to-face. I am eternally thankful that my walk with God, my marriage, my family, and our work as missionaries bears something of the light of Bill Ury's face.

Billy Coppedge, PhD
Missionary
Africa

Dr. Bill Ury possesses the unique ability to grasp the profound and communicate its beauty, all without sanitizing the deep mysteries that lay at the heart of our faith. His gifting in this area is simply second to none. Under his rigorous tutelage, scores of people have been equipped and emboldened to take the gospel of Jesus to the ends of the Earth and for this, we are forever grateful for his heart and life. I could go on and speak of his wit and charm or his genuine concern for his students and their futures. I could write volumes about the impact Dr. Ury has in my ministry as an Anglican priest or the way in which his teachings permeate almost every area of my theological and biblical interpretation. I could do that. But as profound as those things surely are, his most precious gift to me has been to model a husband and father worthy of imitation. In this regard, he is quite simply, second to none. Dr. Ury may have taught me how to think theologically but watching him passionately love his wife and serve the Lord with her by his side, taught me more about the sacrament of marriage than any lecture I've ever attended. Seeing his children and grandchildren, adore and follow the Lord Jesus with their whole hearts, gave me hope that my family tree could be marked by redemption, rather than disaster.

The time I spent under Dr. Ury's brilliant tutelage was marked by scores of astonishing insights. His teachings help me apprehend the Lord and to understand God's hope and intention for us, in a way I never dreamed. But Dr. Ury never provided an insight into the heart of the Lord more profound than to see his heart for his wife and children.

Dr. Ury is a great teacher. But he is an even better father and husband.

Charles Humphrey, Associate Priest

Christ the Redeemer Anglican Church

Ft. Worth, Texas

The concept of God as our loving, heavenly Father can be exceedingly difficult for many people to envision. For me, it has been the easiest and most profound picture of my life. When I think about why I love Jesus, there are many factors, but nothing that exceeds the love and life of my earthly father, Bill Ury. I'm currently 35 years into this life, and I still cannot believe I get the joy and honor of being his daughter. As a mother to four young children, I am also beginning to understand how closely our children watch us and how impossible it is to hide your sin and true self from the people you live with. As this reality continues to sink deeper into my own life, I am also more in awe of the holy love I have witnessed and seen truly lived out every day of my life in my dad.

My father is a brilliant, biblical scholar and theologian, but frankly, there are a lot of really intelligent people in the world. What strikes everyone who has ever encountered Bill, is that he has let the knowledge and ideas go deep into his heart and that has produced true Life. In fact, these are not words and ideas to him. This is a Person. A Person he knows and seeks and has invited daily into his heart and mind and life. And while his vocation has included much study, writing, and speaking — as his child, those things don't mean a lot to me. Rather, it is that his knowledge of this Person, the Triune God, has seeped deep into his bones and consumed his whole being and pours forth from him in a profound, flooding love. A holy love which I've heard him preach about 1000 times, but infinitely more importantly have seen him live every single day of my life. Truly, every single day.

From my perspective, holy love is watching my father change hundreds of his grand-babies' diapers. It's always being the last person to get food and then the moment a child is restless being the first one to offer to walk with them outside. It's driving an old minivan for the last 25+ years, and if he's ever even noticed it, we surely don't know. He has always had this ability to see beyond, even above, the material parts of life.

And yet at the same time, I'm not sure I've ever seen anyone love life more. The pure delight in his eyes when talking to a child. The crazy love of comedy and the desire to laugh as much as possible (the best laugh in the world). How much he really loves food. And travel. And books and movies. Just soaks in all the good stuff.

When I look at my father's life, I know this is most certainly not a life that he "just tried a little harder" into. Rather, I've watched how abiding in Jesus really does produce the most beautiful fruit. And with each passing year I'm increasingly grateful that I get to be a tiny piece of that vine.

JoAnna Ury Pittman, Homeschooling Mother of Four Children
Bill Ury's First Born Child
Raleigh, NC

Too often I have taken for granted the fact that I was raised by Bill Ury. If you've had the privilege of meeting him, you know he lives with a passionate love for Jesus. It radiates from him. Not only does my dad love Jesus but he truly knows Him, and his life has been changed by Jesus' holy love.

I remember as a young kid wondering why people were so drawn to my dad. One of my favorite memories is from when I was ten years old and my family decided to build an addition onto the back of our home, in true Ury do-it-yourself fashion. Over those several weeks of construction, what started off as a small group of helpers turned into *dozens*. It was incredible to see so many people from our different circles surrounding us with their support: hammering, painting, laying cement, installing windows. As I got older, I realized the "why" behind that renovation crew that loved our family. Those sweet people in some way or another had been touched by my dad's love. They were giving back. My dad had seen them with Jesus' eyes. He knew them and had served them. He'd listened to them. He'd prayed for them. He'd carried burdens with them. Everyone there knew his love was unique. They'd interacted with Holy Love.

As his little girl, I witnessed this love throughout my life. I was told more times than many young girls how loved and cherished I was by my dad. He still says, "Hi, my beautiful" when he hugs me. I can't deny that while growing up I also had a healthy fear of my dad. The worst days were days when my siblings and I were in trouble, and we had to "wait for dad to come home" to hear our punishment. As I got older, my boyfriend (and now husband) also gained a reasonable fear of my dad. There was something about his love that desired to protect me and always wanted what was best for me. He and I had some painful conversations and disagreements about his approach. Instead of being lazy and backing off, he stood firm in what he knew was right for me. We'd fight for days, but in the end, I'd run back to his arms, always open, for forgiveness and safety.

I am now in my thirties, and I am still learning about holy love, but I'm further along than I would be without the honor of knowing my dad. His life looks a little different now, and it's usually his sticky grandbabies that are swarming him rather than his students. He is still someone that we all want more of. We are drawn to him, and his love is a place of comfort for us. We've all been changed by the way he lives and loves. If you've bumped into my dad, you've bumped into Jesus. Because of my dad, we've tasted Holy Love.

Maighdlin Ury Hauser, Head of People and Talent

Will Reed

Bill Ury's Second Born Child

Wendell, NC

My dad's whole life has been committed to helping others understand the holy love of God, whether that was in formal settings like church services and seminary lectures or informal environments like our dinner table, family trips, and coffee dates. I have listened to hundreds of hours of my dad's teaching, and yet I still sit on the edge of my chair whenever he is about to start speaking, notebook and pen ready. I will forever have his voice in the back of my mind repeating "Trinitarian reality", and "Mutual, other-oriented, self-giving love". These words and ideas not only shaped my theology but also my everyday reality because my dad not only taught them but lived them, and I have been the recipient and experienced them tangibly. Just like grace always works, I was brought up in and shaped by holy love without even understanding what was happening, and the Lord drew me to Himself through my dad's life of holy love.

When I think about how my dad embodies holy love, the word "generous" comes to mind. There is not one area of his life that he withholds from other people. He is generous with his money: always giving gifts, offering his "tithe" to us, and taking us on dates. Even when we were younger and money was tight, I never sensed him withholding from his family. If he had anything to give, he always shared it. My dad is generous with his time: dropping everything and babysitting so I can finish a school paper, finding and installing a washer in our new house, helping me research for school or answering my theological questions. I believe you can tell a lot about a person's heart by the way they act around food. My dad is generous with his food: he will watch the babies first so the moms can eat, he will offer you his food if your order was not what you wanted, he always wants to share his meals, and always makes sure everyone else ate enough, saying "Take mine, please, I don't want it". My dad is generous with his words and affection:

you will never have a conversation with him that revolves around him because he always asks questions and wants you to feel loved and known. He is generous with his encouragement and doesn't withhold his affection. He bravely risks rejection trying to connect with strangers because he does not exist for himself. The words that he offers are refined by his desire to be holy, because he never gossips and is willing to admit mistakes. Lastly, he is generous with his love for life! His genuine joy and laughter are so irresistible and compelling that everyone wants to be in the same room as him.

These examples and many others demonstrate that my dad not only believes in and teaches about the holy love of God, but that he is also being transformed into a person of holy love.

Meredith Ury Bauman, MDiv.

Bill Ury's Third Born Child

Knightdale, NC

I have just become a dad. For less than a year I have been able to share this title with my own son. A man being called a "dad" is not so hard. It has initial feelings of pride and accomplishment attached to it, without even knowing too much about the person. When I find out that a man whom I have met has kids, I immediately feel highly about them. The title is good to me because my dad is good to me. The title never leaves us either.

Another cornerstone of being a dad that I have noticed is the way dads then look at their kids. They watch them, guard them, look out for them. But there is a certain look that carries much more weight. This is when all our attention is on them, with no expectation or agenda, but just blissfully holding them in our eyes. The past messes or loud voices, the future hang-ups, or expenses; none of those belong to this child. Sometimes, I can only see the one who belongs to me. I can see Foster because my dad saw me. He still sees me.

He also speaks to me. Dads have words that no other humans possess. They might be spelled the same, sound the same, or be defined the same for every person, but in the mouth of a dad they mean almost infinitely more. Almost. Like they are hinting that, one day, we will hear soft, deep words that shake our knees and water our eyes with the purest fear and comfort. My son does not yet have his words, but I have mine. I have this power in my voice because my dad gave it to me. He has also heard me use this power in evil ways. I abused it in my lies and my arrogance. It has done what I wanted it to do, but what I had been given was not faulty. I have used my vision much the same. I was able to blissfully contemplate evil as though it were for my good, with depth and precision. My eyes were damaged, and my voice trembled.

But dads also hear the weakest cries. They also go towards the shrillest ones; the cries that most people stay away from, because the reasons for them can be brutal and they disrupt rest. I never knew that a person could translate cries to mean so many different things. But having my son has taught me differently. In a short time, I have found myself able to know my son's voice well. I can hear him because my dad has never ignored my cry, whether stifled, hidden, or cacophonous.

Nothing I had in my voice, my eyes, or my reputation was too much for him. He is my father, and I am his son. His love for me is good and true. He has never given up on crafting his love towards me in Holiness from the Father.

Seth Nelson Ury, Latin and Classics Teacher
The First Academy
Bill Ury's Fourth Born Child
Orlando, FL